KEY ISSUES
IN
INTERNATIONAL
MONETARY REFORM

BUSINESS ECONOMICS AND FINANCE
a series of monographs and textbooks

Executive Editor
Arthur B. Laffer
Department of Economics
University of Chicago
Graduate School of Business
Chicago, Illinois

Co-Editor
Gene C. Uselton
Department of Economics
Texas Tech University
College of Arts and Sciences
Lubbock, Texas

Volume 1
Common Globe or Global Commons: Population
Regulation and Income Distribution   John C. G. Boot

Volume 2
Lags in the Effects of Monetary Policy: A Nonparametric
Analysis   Gene C. Uselton

Volume 3
Demand for Money in Israel   Lewis Mandell

Volume 4
Key Issues in International Monetary
Reform   Edited by Randall Hinshaw

Other Volumes in Preparation.

KEY ISSUES IN INTERNATIONAL MONETARY REFORM

Edited by RANDALL HINSHAW

Claremont Graduate School, Claremont, California

MARCEL DEKKER, INC.   NEW YORK

COPYRIGHT © 1975 by MARCEL DEKKER, INC.

ALL RIGHTS RESERVED. Neither this book nor any part may be reproduced or transmitted in any form or by any means, electronic or mechanical, including photocopying, microfilming, and recording, or by any information storage and retrieval system, without permission in writing from the publisher.

MARCEL DEKKER, INC.
270 Madison Avenue, New York, New York 10016

LIBRARY OF CONGRESS CATALOG CARD NUMBER: 75-18963
ISBN: 0-8247-6324-6
Current printing (last digit):
10 9 8 7 6 5 4 3 2 1

PRINTED IN THE UNITED STATES OF AMERICA

CONTENTS

     CONTRIBUTORS   v

     FOREWORD   vii
         Barnaby C. Keeney

I.   INTRODUCTION   1
         Randall Hinshaw

II.   ISSUES AND CHOICES   11
         Lord Robbins

III.   OFFICIAL PERSPECTIVES   29
         Frank A. Southard, Jr.
         Robert Solomon
         Guenther Schleiminger

IV.   INTERNATIONAL MONETARY REFORM:
     EXCHANGE-RATE ISSUES   43
         Robert A. Mundell and Conference Members

V.   KEY ISSUES IN THE DESIGN OF REFORM   71
         John Parke Young and Conference Members

VI.   THE DESIGN OF REFORM: OTHER VIEWS   103
         Gottfried Haberler and Conference Members

VII.   TRADE ISSUES IN INTERNATIONAL
     MONETARY REFORM   121
         Isaiah Frank and Conference Members

iv   CONTENTS

VIII. KEY ISSUES: THE PROBLEM OF
       CAPITAL MOVEMENTS   133
          Richard N. Cooper and Conference Members

  IX. CONCLUDING REFLECTIONS   145
          Lord Robbins

       INDEXES   159

CONTRIBUTORS

SVEN W. ARNDT, Fellow, Crown College, University of California, Santa Cruz

JAGDISH BHAGWATI, Professor of Economics, Massachusetts Institute of Technology; Editor, Journal of International Economics

ROY BLOUGH, Member, President's Council of Economic Advisers, 1950-52; Director of International Economic Studies, Committee for Economic Development

ROBERT W. CLOWER, Professor of Economics, University of California, Los Angeles

RICHARD N. COOPER, Professor of Economics and Provost, Yale University

GORDON K. DOUGLASS, Chairman, Department of Economics, Pomona College

JOHN EXTER, Senior Vice President (retired), First National City Bank of New York

ISAIAH FRANK, William L. Clayton Professor of International Economics, School of Advanced International Studies, The Johns Hopkins University

C. DILLON GLENDINNING, Treasurer (retired), Mobil International Oil Company; Deputy Director, Office of International Finance, U. S. Treasury Department, 1950-57

GOTTFRIED HABERLER, Galen L. Stone Professor of International Trade Emeritus, Harvard University; Resident Scholar, American Enterprise Institute

SEYMOUR E. HARRIS, Littauer Professor of Political Economy Emeritus, Harvard University

CONTRIBUTORS

Sir ROY HARROD, Oxford University
RANDALL HINSHAW, Professor of Economics, Claremont Graduate School
CONRAD C. JAMISON, Vice President and Economist, Security Pacific National Bank
PETER B. KENEN, Walker Professor of Economics and International Finance, Princeton University
ARTHUR B. LAFFER, Consultant to the Secretary of the Treasury; the Economist, U. S. Office of Management and Budget, 1970-72
FRITZ MACHLUP, Walker Professor of Economics and International Finance Emeritus, Princeton University
ROBERT A. MUNDELL, Professor of Economics, Columbia University
ROBERT W. OLIVER, Professor of Economics, California Institute of Technology
Lord ROBBINS, Chairman, Court of Governors, London School of Economics
WALTER S. SALANT, Senior Fellow, The Brookings Institution
GUENTHER SCHLEIMINGER, Executive Director for Germany, International Monetary Fund
WILSON E. SCHMIDT, Chairman, Department of Economics, Virginia Polytechnic Institute; Deputy Assistant Secretary of the Treasury, 1970-72
TIBOR SCITOVSKY, Professor of Economics, Stanford University
LEONARD S. SILK, Editorial Board, New York Times
ROBERT SOLOMON, Vice Chairman, Deputies of the Commitee of Twenty; Adviser to the Board, Board of Governors of the Federal Reserve System
FRANK A. SOUTHARD, JR., Deputy Managing Director, International Monetary Fund
WILLARD L. THORP, Assistant Secretary of State for Economic Affairs, 1947-52
ROBERT TRIFFIN, Frederick William Beinecke Professor of Economics, Yale University
HENRY C. WALLICH, Seymour H. Knox Professor of Economics, Yale University; Senior Consultant to the Secretary of the Treasury
JOHN PARKE YOUNG, former Chief, Division of International Finance, U. S. Department of State

FOREWORD

The fourth Bologna-Claremont international monetary conference was sponsored by the Claremont Graduate School at Claremont in mid-February 1973. The Claremont Colleges, particularly Scripps College, cooperated in the venture in various ways.

As had been the case in the three previous conferences, a carefully selected group of international monetary experts was invited from academic and research institutions, and from governments and private organizations. Willard L. Thorp chaired, and Lord Robbins moderated the proceedings. The Johns Hopkins University Bologna Center, which has sponsored alternate conferences in this series, was represented by C. Grove Haines, its founder, and Simon Serfaty, its director.

Professor Randall Hinshaw served as rapporteur, and this volume is his work as editor. Professor Hinshaw was likewise responsible for the careful prior organization of the conference and for its smooth operation. But for him, the conference's total proceedings would not have been subsequently known to persons who were not there, and the conference probably would not have been held.

Seldom has an event of this sort been so appropriately timed or titled. "Key Issues in International Monetary Reform" were the key issues in February 1973, and events lent an urgency to the proceedings that is rare in academic life—even when academicians interact fruitfully with men of affairs who are directly involved.

We are deeply indebted to the John Randolph Haynes and Dora Haynes Foundation and to Security Pacific National Bank for their financial support and their hospitality. We are grateful to Mr. and Mrs. John Parke Young, who entertained both conferees and camp followers at their gracious home. Numerous Claremont people assisted Professor Hinshaw in planning and staging the meetings.

BARNABY C. KEENEY
President
Claremont Graduate School

KEY ISSUES
IN
INTERNATIONAL
MONETARY REFORM

I. INTRODUCTION

Randall Hinshaw

Except for the Introduction, this book is an edited tape recording of a conference on "Key Issues in International Monetary Reform" held at Claremont, California in mid-February 1973. The conference, which was sandwiched between two international monetary crises, was the fourth in a series of biennial meetings alternately sponsored by the Johns Hopkins University Center in Bologna, Italy, and Claremont Graduate School. The series has been conceived as an effort to bring together leading experts in academic, official, and banking circles for deeply probing dialogues on international monetary problems of foremost current interest. Unlike the procedure at most gatherings of this kind, no formal papers are circulated in advance, the effort being rather to generate a spontaneous exchange of views.

It would be pointless to attempt here a summary of the 1973 dialogue—a task elegantly performed by Lord Robbins, the conference Moderator, in his closing remarks, reproduced in Chapter IX. It may be helpful to the nonspecialist, however, to offer a bit of postwar background and a brief postscript; the specialist may prefer to turn immediately to Chapter II.

In a broad sense, the entire postwar period has been involved in international monetary reform of one kind or another. The legacy of the Great Depression and World War II was a complete breakdown of normal international monetary and trade arrangements, and the monetary goal of the early postwar years was a return to convertibility of the major non-dollar currencies, the dollar being already convertible not only into other currencies but also—for foreign central banks—into gold. Convertibility of the Western European currencies into each other was achieved under the European Payments Union (1950-58), an ingenious transitional institution which, on a regional scale, borrowed some of the main features of the Keynes Clearing Union proposal of 1943. The more difficult objective of convertibility into the dollar was attained at the end of 1958 under the European Monetary Agreement, a technical arrangement which achieved the desired result by the simple device of making the U. S. dollar the "intervention currency"—i. e., the currency to be used by participating central banks for keeping exchange rates within the narrow limits established by the International Monetary Fund.

Under the IMF rules then prevailing, a member country was required to keep its exchange rate within a range not exceeding 1 percent above or below the official parity. Central banks, if they wished, could maintain a narrower range of fluctuations, but were required to "intervene" when the IMF floor or ceiling had been reached. Under the European Monetary Agreement, such intervention took the form of central bank sales or purchases of U. S. dollars.

For example, if the French franc were weak, the Bank of France was obligated to sell dollars in exchange for all francs offered by the foreign-exchange market whenever the dollar price of the franc had dropped to the lower limit. In this way, the foreign-exchange market was always assured of a supply of dollars with which to meet the needs of importers and others wishing to make authorized dollar payments. In the opposite case, if the franc were strong, the Bank of France was obligated to buy dollars from the foreign-exchange market in exchange for francs whenever the dollar price of the franc had risen to the upper limit. Any unwanted dollars thus flowing to the Bank of France could be exchanged for U. S. gold, and this option was frequently used. The result of these arrangements was that Western Europe, as many observers pointed out, was in effect on a "dollar standard," whereas the United States was on what was often called a "gold standard for central banks." In several respects, the system was decidedly unsymmetrical, and the issue of "symmetry" was to attract considerable attention at the 1973 conference.

The return to convertibility, far from ushering in a utopian era, introduced difficulties and dilemmas which were soon to become the basis for a new drive for international monetary reform. Among the earliest to be concerned was Robert Triffin, a Yale professor who earlier had been one of the leading architects of the European Payments Union. In his book, Gold and the Dollar Crisis, published in 1960, Triffin expressed alarm about the instability of a system based mainly on gold and the U. S. dollar, which together accounted for more than four-fifths of international monetary reserves. With the expanding volume of international trade, it was of major importance, under a regime of pegged exchange rates, that monetary reserves grow at a reasonably even rate—a rate which was neither so high as to cause global inflation nor so low as to create a deflationary drag. During the late 1950s and early 1960s, aggregate reserves were expanding at a reasonable rate, but only because of the chronic U. S. payments deficit, which was mainly "settled" in dollars.

With persuasive logic, Triffin argued that this entirely unplanned and unforeseen mechanism of reserve expansion was inherently capricious and unstable. If the U. S. payments deficit were to end, reserve expansion in the form of dollars would end; even if the U. S. deficit continued, reserve expansion could end or be reversed if central banks were to convert an increased fraction of their dollar holdings into gold. The United States in any case was losing gold, and it was only a matter of time until foreign central banks would be seriously concerned about how long their dollars would remain convertible into gold. At the time Triffin was writing, U. S. gold holdings were still about twice as large as the dollar holdings of foreign central banks, but the ratio was rapidly declining.

Thus the system contained the seeds of its own destruction. By the end of 1964, U. S. holdings of monetary gold, at $15.5 billion, had fallen below the dollar holdings of foreign central banks ($15.8 billion). But the U. S. balance of payments, while continuing to be in overall deficit, was still characterized by a large trade surplus; indeed, the trade surplus attained a record level of $6.8 billion in 1964. Dollars held by the foreign private sector (by foreign business firms, commercial banks, and individuals) continued to rise, and since this increase was entirely voluntary—a response to the expanding need for dollar working balances—the dollar was still widely regarded as in basically good shape.

Indeed, matters were going so smoothly in the mid-1960s that it took a trained sharp eye to see any handwriting on the wall. In marked contrast to the "double-digit" inflation of the 1970s, the U. S. wholesale price level remained almost perfectly flat from 1958 through 1964, the index rounding to 100, on a 1958 base, for seven years in a row! During this period, the U. S. unemployment rate steadily declined, falling below 4 percent in 1966. And by both earlier and later standards, the U. S. payments deficits were modest; on an official-settlements basis, the annual deficit was less than $2 billion for the four years 1962-65, and in 1966 the deficit was replaced by a small surplus.

In view of later developments, it now seems strange that the international monetary problem attracting most attention in the mid-1960s was the apparent threat of an impending shortage of international liquidity. The two main forms of monetary reserve—gold and the dollar—both appeared to be approaching some kind of limit; indeed, both actually declined in 1966, the the decline in dollars reflecting the U. S. payments surplus and the decline in gold reflecting a growing movement from the official to the private sector.

It was against this background—so different from the world of the 1970s—that the first conference in the present series was held in Bologna in January 1967. Although the original purpose of the conference was to consider the role of gold in international monetary reform, the discussion quickly broadened to a re-examination, in the setting of the mid-1960s, of the major alternatives to existing arrangements. The conference was fortunate in having as members three of the foremost advocates of reform: Robert Triffin, author of the celebrated "Triffin Plan"; Jacques Rueff, the eminent French economist; and Edward M. Bernstein, who earlier had been a leading official of the U. S. Treasury and of the International Monetary Fund. These three experts all favored a system under which exchange rates would be fixed rather than flexible, and under which monetary reserves would grow at an appropriate rate, but their views on the form in which reserves should be held and on the mechanism of reserve expansion differed sharply.

Triffin's prescription, first offered several years earlier, was to end the role of the dollar as an international monetary reserve. He proposed, instead, to convert the International Monetary Fund into a world central bank in which the various national central banks would hold most of their reserves in the form of convertible demand deposits. Central banks would initially obtain such deposits in exchange for their existing holdings of dollars, other reserve currencies, and an agreed fraction of their gold. To achieve an appropriate expansion of reserves, the reformed IMF would be empowered to create deposits by making loans to countries in payments difficulties and by buying government securities.

Although emphatically agreeing with Triffin that the role of the dollar as a reserve currency should be ended, Rueff favored a radically different approach to reform. He proposed that the official dollar price of gold should be sharply raised and that the resulting increase in the dollar value of U. S. gold should be used to reimburse foreign central banks for their dollar holdings, leaving the United States no worse off than before. Under this reform, international balances would henceforth be settled exclusively in gold, the dollar would no longer be used as a reserve currency, and the United States would therefore no longer be in the privileged position of being able, in Rueff's words, to run "deficits without tears." The higher gold price, in Rueff's opinion, would stimulate gold production sufficiently to assure an appropriate growth of international monetary reserves, which, under his scheme, would be solely in the form of gold.

Of the three, Bernstein's approach was the most conservative in the sense that it involved the least interference with existing arrangements. Bernstein did not wish to replace the dollar as a monetary reserve, but he did feel that central bank holdings of dollars should not continue to grow. In his view, the U. S. payments deficit should come to an end (as it then appeared to be doing), and future additions to international monetary reserves should take place, on a carefully planned basis, in the form of a newly created international reserve asset, or "reserve unit," which, though not convertible into gold, would be endowed with all the international monetary attributes of gold, including, in particular, the capacity to settle international balances.

Although not explicitly presented as a reform, a fourth view was eloquently offered by another distinguished conference member, Professor James Meade of Cambridge University. Meade felt strongly that the primary problem was not the lack of adequate international liquidity but the lack of an effective international adjustment mechanism. In this respect, he was in hearty agreement with Jacques Rueff. His prescription, however, was very different. Meade believed that what was needed was an adjustment mechanism which would promote international balance while at the same time enabling a country to pursue enlightened domestic policies, including the maintenance of a stable domestic price level—a mechanism which would protect a country from inflationary or deflationary pressures originating from abroad. This objective could be achieved, in his opinion, through greater flexibility of exchange rates—an approach already receiving wide support in academic circles. Although Meade's prescription was on a different wave-length from those of Triffin, Rueff, and Bernstein, all of which were based on fixed (but alterable) exchange rates, his plea for an effective international adjustment mechanism made a deep impression; indeed, international adjustment became the theme of the second biennial conference, held at Claremont in March 1969.

No effort was made to reach a consensus at the 1967 conference, but it is not surprising that the Bernstein approach became the basis, later in the year, for a reform in the international monetary system. Official thinking along such lines had been proceeding for several years, and at the annual meeting of the International Monetary Fund in Rio de Janeiro, agreement was reached on the creation of a new reserve unit in the form of "special drawing rights" (SDRs). The SDR was designed as a reserve asset which could be used for any of the international monetary purposes served by gold, dollars, or other reserve currencies—including repayment of borrowings from the Fund. Issued in annual amounts to be determined by the Fund, the SDR (originally at parity with the U. S. dollar) was intended to assure an appropriate growth in aggregate reserves in a world where other reserve assets were expected either not to grow at all or to grow at an inadequate rate. SDR allocations were to be in proportion to IMF quotas, and the initial allocations were made for a three-year period in annual installments; the first installment of $3.4 billion was made on January 1, 1970, with installments of about $3 billion each at the beginning of 1971 and of 1972.

It is tempting to speculate on how this reform would have worked if the U. S. balance of payments had remained in a position of overall balance or of modest surplus. Ironically, however, the addition to global reserves in the form of SDRs occurred at a time when, because of dollar weakness, central bank holdings of dollars suddenly began to increase at an explosive rate. In 1970, the U. S. balance of payments, on an official-settlements basis, revealed a deficit of $9.8 billion—almost three times the previous record. The deficit reflected an unmistakable decline of confidence in the dollar associated with growing evidence of serious U. S. inflation. For the first time in two decades, private foreign dollar balances, which had been rising steadily since 1950, showed a sharp decline—from $28.2 billion at the end of 1969 to $21.8 billion at the end of 1970. The dollars thus dumped by the private sector went directly into foreign central banks, which had to buy them to keep the dollar price of their currencies from rising above the agreed ceilings. For some countries, the inflow of dollars added greatly to central bank problems in coping with inflationary pressures, and on June 1, 1970, the Bank of Canada, whose holdings of U. S. dollars had increased by 45 percent during the first five months of the year, "ceased to assure" that the Canadian dollar would remain within the IMF limits. The Canadian dollar thereupon promptly floated through the ceiling, and by the end of the year had risen more than 6 percent above its IMF parity.

It was against this disturbing background that the third biennial conference was held in Bologna in April 1971. The theme was "inflation as a global problem," inflation for which the United States was—with much evidence—widely regarded as largely responsible because of its dominant position in the world economy and because of its unique situation of being able to "export" its own accelerating inflation by means of "deficits without tears."

In the meantime, the deficit was reaching alarming proportions. On an official-settlements basis, the U. S. payments deficit in 1971 amounted to the startling figure of $29.8 billion. Of this total, more than nine-tenths was financed by an increase in central bank dollar holdings, which more than doubled during the year. The deficit reflected, among other things, immense transfers of short-term capital to countries, such as Germany and Japan, whose currencies were expected to appreciate in relation to the dollar. Understandably, central banks were distressed at having to make such enormous dollar purchases, and during the first seven and a half months of 1971 they converted more than $800 million into U. S. gold. The United States, alarmed at the possibility of rapidly losing the remainder of its gold, withdrew the convertibility privilege on August 15, 1971.

8   INTRODUCTION

It will not be necessary to discuss here the turbulent events between mid-August 1971 and the Claremont conference of mid-February 1973, as this background is admirably provided in Chapter III by Frank A. Southard, Jr., then Deputy Managing Director of the International Monetary Fund. The 1973 conference came immediately after an international monetary crisis that was resolved the preceding week by a second devaluation of the dollar; indeed, if the conference had been held a week earlier, several participants from official circles would have been unable to attend.

The purpose of the 1973 meeting was to take a new look at reform issues in the light of the radically changed situation. One thing was clear: the big reform of the 1960s—the SDR—was irrelevant to the international monetary problems of the early 1970s. Reserve creation was clearly not the problem in a world in which reserves in the form of dollars had more than tripled in the preceding two and a half years. Lamentably, as Robert Triffin had pointed out in Bologna in 1971, the SDR had been brought into being without doing anything to "clean up the past."

Under the skillful chairmanship of Willard L. Thorp, the conference dialogue falls neatly into chapters. Following the introductory remarks of the Chairman, Chapter II presents the opening address of Lord Robbins, the Moderator, setting out the issues and alternatives as he viewed them in early 1973. This was the only formal paper delivered at the conference. The remainder of the first session, reproduced in Chapter III, was reserved for statements by three prominent officials: the previously mentioned statement by Mr. Southard on the events of the preceding year and a half; a statement on current official thinking by Robert Solomon, Vice Chairman of the Deputies of the "Committee of Twenty" (formally the "Committee on Reform of the International Monetary System and Related Issues"); and a statement by Guenther Schleiminger, IMF Executive Director for Germany, offering a German perspective on reform issues.

The balance of the conference was devoted to four general topics: exchange-rate questions in connection with monetary reform, presented in Chapter IV; issues related to the "design" of reform, presented in Chapters V and VI; trade issues in relation to reform, presented in Chapter VII; and problems arising from massive crisis-producing international capital movements, presented in Chapter VIII. In each of these areas, there was considerable disagreement both on matters of analysis and on matters of policy. The thinking on reform revealed wide differences of opinion on such questions as the role of rules—versus discretion—in international adjustment; the appropriate degree of flexibility (or of inflexibility) in exchange rates; the role, if any, of gold in future international monetary arrangements; and the future role of the SDR—including particularly the question of whether the rules for allocation should be changed in such a way as to bestow a larger share, or perhaps all, of new SDRs on the developing countries. It was clear that official thinking was a long way from consensus on these matters and in any case was on a different wave-length from such proposals as the Triffin Plan in its various versions or John Parke Young's suggestion, presented in Chapter V, for an international currency available to the public as well as to central banks.

The conference dialogue is summarized and commented upon by Lord Robbins in his characteristically judicious concluding observations, reproduced in Chapter IX.

The 1973 conference was promptly followed by a new speculative attack on the dollar which culminated in action that, at least for the time being, marked the end of the "Bretton Woods system" of pegged exchange rates. In March, as a means of coping with the new crisis, those Common Market countries that were not already floating their currencies agreed to a common float against the dollar. They were joined informally by Norway and Sweden. Other major currencies floating independently included the Swiss franc, the Japanese yen, and, as previously mentioned, the Canadian dollar. Under these arrangements, the dollar held steady for a few weeks, and then, influenced by the Watergate upheaval, depreciated sharply.

By apparently eliminating crises of the kind that plagued the early 1970s, the regime of floating rates has greatly reduced the impetus for early agreement on international monetary reform. Moreover, for countries whose currencies have appreciated—countries, such as Switzerland and Germany, which have been more successful than others in avoiding domestically produced inflation—the floating-rate regime, by reducing external inflationary pressures, has undoubtedly been a blessing.

For most other countries, however, the story has been very different. This is notably true of the United States, which, prior to the general floating, was able to "export" much of its own inflation. It can no longer do this, but, instead, immediately suffers whenever the dollar declines in terms of other currencies.

A decline in the dollar promptly raises U. S. prices, not only of imports and of import-competing U. S. production, but also of "exportables"—notably farm products, some of which are exported but most of which are consumed by Americans. The price increases occur immediately in the case of primary products and more slowly in the case of U. S. manufactured goods made from primary products, but a large part of the rise in the U. S. price level in the 1970s is directly due to the dollar depreciation—including two formal devaluations—that has occurred since 1969.

Of course, the dollar depreciation, while the immediate cause of widespread price increases, is itself due to U. S. inflation, as Milton Friedman and others have properly insisted. But precisely because floating exchange rates do not provide any kind of balance-of-payments constraint, they enable inflationary policies to continue indefinitely—with the sky the limit unless effective action intervenes.

What has been said of the United States applies even more to many other countries, including the United Kingdom, where a floating pound has permitted inflationary policies that could not have continued on such a scale if it had been necessary to defend a fixed parity.

Thus it is difficult, at least for this observer, to escape the conclusion that, whatever its virtues during a turbulent period, the present regime of floating rates has, on balance, a strongly inflationary bias—and that it will continue to have such a bias until political leaders become far more concerned than they are now with the direct price-boosting effects of currency depreciation. If this conclusion is correct, it clearly would be folly to assume that there is no longer an urgent need for international monetary reform—reform which, if it is to be fruitful, will require great wisdom in dealing with the complex and perplexing issues explored in the ensuing pages.

II. ISSUES AND CHOICES

Lord Robbins

Chairman WILLARD L. THORP: A number of us have attended all of the previous conferences in the Bologna-Claremont series, but there are some who have not had that experience, so I will take a moment to indicate briefly the matters that have been covered in our past meetings.

The 1967 conference dealt largely with the role of gold in the international monetary system. We had representatives from South Africa and other people interested in the production and use of gold, and I would say that since that time some of the developments there foreseen and solutions there suggested have taken place. I cite this merely to indicate the relevance of these conferences.

The 1969 conference was concerned with the problem of international adjustment. Since that time, there have been changes in the foreign-exchange mechanism along lines which were then explored. By late 1970, it had become clear that inflation was no longer confined to particular countries, but was virtually worldwide, so our 1971 meeting investigated the extraordinary phenomenon of global inflation. The widespread character of this economic behavior suggested that the problem must have something to do with international monetary matters, and our conference on that subject turned out to be particularly significant.

In each case, the conference has dealt with a currently disturbing problem in the international monetary field. While I would not be so bold as to suggest that our discussions have resolved the issues, there is no doubt in my mind that discussions among experts, including some in positions of special responsibility, cannot help but move us on toward solutions. These conferences have undoubtedly contributed to the state of knowledge concerning the new setting in which monetary problems appear. Sometimes, it has been the disclosure of some fact or condition, like the inelasticity of gold production or double counting in Eurodollar statistics. Sometimes, it has been the analysis of forces at work to which economic theory has given little attention, such as the international flow of funds. In any event, what I do wish to emphasize is the extraordinary relevance to current policy issues which these conferences have enjoyed.

As you can see, all of our conferences have been centered on the question of what changes are necessary in order to have a more effective international monetary system. Now in 1973, the fourth conference in the series is to focus on the subject of monetary reform. We must attempt to define and consider the key issues which must be settled. I think it is important to remember that, at our last conference, Lord Robbins in his concluding observations warned us that these problems would be resolved in political centers and not by economists. He said, in effect, that international monetary reform is essentially a political problem, by which I think he meant that reform would have to be negotiated among governments and that solutions would have to be found that were satisfactory to different governments having different interests. It is also important to recall that, immediately following Lord Robbins' remarks, Bob Mundell made the effective point that, even though monetary reform is a political problem, this fact does not relieve the economist of his duty to do his best to analyze the situation and to give advice on what appears to be the wisest course of action.

International monetary reform, as we all know, has been the subject of extended study elsewhere. Other conferences have dealt with the matter, and the directors of the International Monetary Fund have recently released a rather detailed report entitled "Reform of the International Monetary System." Those of you who have read it may have been impressed by the fact that, on most of the matters discussed, the conclusion is reached that further study is needed. One might almost get the impression that the Monetary Fund has an eagerness to establish itself as a permanent research organization, which to some extent it is. In any case, it is quite clear that, as far as the Fund is concerned, these problems are not simple, the facts are not always clear, and international agreement is conspicuously lacking.

I should also mention that the United States, through Secretary of the Treasury Shultz, has presented in rough detail its program for monetary reform. To some extent, it parallels the Fund report. Perhaps the biggest difference is that the Monetary Fund adds a chapter on financial flows as being so disturbing as to call for special action, whereas Secretary Shultz gives emphasis to the trade field as requiring action. But both reports present very much the same set of problems.

I think we all would agree that something is seriously wrong. These recurring monetary crises are highly disturbing, and solutions that are reached in a crisis atmosphere are not necessarily the most reasonable ones. Thus there is a real need for a meeting such as this, in which these matters can be probed as deeply and as objectively as humanly possible.

Just a word about the ground rules. I hope that members will realize that everyone around the table has a fairly advanced background on our conference theme. Among our members are a considerable number of professional talkers, including myself, who can expand on any subject. But that is not the ability we most need, and it is probably a sign of incapacity if one can't make his point to a group like this in five minutes or less.

And now to our Moderator. In trying to find out just what his duties are, I looked up the word in the dictionary and found a whole series of definitions. One which seemed somewhat appropriate is that he is "the presiding officer at a town meeting." But since this is hardly a town meeting, I have chosen another definition, which is as follows: "an arrangement for supplying oil to the wick in a kind of lamp." This obviously is the first step in the process of shedding light. I now call on Lord Robbins.

Lord ROBBINS: You don't make things any easier, my dear Willard, by the proscriptions that you have laid down in the last few minutes. Among these, I noted with special contrition that you recommended us all to confine our remarks to five minutes, whereas I am under orders from Randall Hinshaw to talk for rather longer than that.

Chairman THORP: His orders take precedence over mine, I assure you.

Lord ROBBINS: As for shedding light, the event will show, but I have no very great confidence that I shall succeed in arousing unanimity. As you reminded us, the last time this group met at Bologna two years ago, the subject of our discussion was inflation from the international point of view. Certainly, that problem has not vanished from the earth, in spite of our deliberations. Even the lower rates of inflation which have been achieved in some parts are still of an order of magnitude which bids fair to reduce the purchasing power of money at a quite alarming speed and to place all cultural institutions at risk, and commercial and private prudence at a discount. And the rate of inflation still prevailing up to a recent date at least in my own country, the United Kingdom, has been such as to be likely to be incompatible in the not very long run with economic or even political stability, let alone progress.

But this time, here at Claremont, our terms of reference are different: not inflation as such but international monetary disorder. Clearly, it would be wrong to suppose that there is a total discontinuity in the universe of discourse. Much, though not all, of the trouble in international monetary relations arises from inflation or, more precisely, from unequal rates of inflation; and doubtless, in the course of our discussions, we shall have to return again and again to this point. But the focus of discussion is different. Since we last met, the dollar has been declared inconvertible; the famous Smithsonian agreement has been broken by the United Kingdom; the structure of the Common Market financial arrangements is in doubt; and this last week there has been yet another of these perplexing international exchange crises. There is no agreement concerning the future rules, if any, of the International Monetary Fund. So there is certainly no paucity of subjects to talk about.

But before doing so, perhaps it is worth asking: Is it worthwhile? Does the presence or absence of order in international monetary relations really matter? After all, on the whole, the world has not done too badly in the last quarter of a century—at any rate, as compared with earlier periods. The world hasn't done as badly as all that even in the last two years. Does the occurrence of these occasional crises mean as much to the world at large as it does to those of us who are professionally concerned with them?

Well, to those who place unlimited faith in self-determination and in laissez-faire in international relations, I suppose the only cause for complaint about the present situation is that it is not sufficiently devoid of vestigial constraints. If only every national authority from the United States to San Salvador would abandon all attempts to maintain orderly relationships between its monetary systems and other systems, then, on this school of thought's point of view, there would be no cause for anxiety about anything. The mechanism of free markets would insure optimal relationships all around. Needless to say, I would not suggest for a moment that anyone in this learned assembly holds such simpliste views. But they are not much of a parody of what I have heard in some not utterly uninfluential quarters at home.

Unfortunately, there is no reason to believe that they are true. I say unfortunately: after all, how splendid it would be if just letting everything free would produce the best of all possible worlds. But I suggest—and I hope in this, at least, to secure agreement—that there are strong empirical grounds, only to be ignored at peril, which suggest that something a little more sophisticated than utter freedom is necessary if international disorder is to be prevented.

In the first place, I suggest that a complete absence of responsibility for fluctuations of rates of exchange is an open door to inflation. By this I don't mean only that it leaves finance ministers freer to print money and pile up deficits without any fear of danger until the downward plunge becomes recognized to be inconvenient. I mean something more than that. I mean that, in the absence of countervailing measures, a downward movement of rates may itself act as an inflationary influence—directly, by its influence on wage and salary demands because of its effect on import prices; indirectly, by its effect in creating an export surplus and thereby changing the relation of income to domestically available goods.

But these, after all, are domestic matters—at any rate, in the first instance. Perhaps I mention them at all only because British experience in this respect has been so vividly impressed on my mind. Much more important would be the specifically international complications of a state of complete laissez-faire.

The first thing that would certainly happen, in the absence of special prohibitions, would be that individuals and corporations in different national areas would start making their contracts in the currencies which were expected to retain or increase their value. We know that this happens already whenever it is not prevented by ferocious penalties. We can be quite sure, therefore, that the state of total freedom desired by the advocates of the system I am considering would almost certainly be accompanied in the weaker areas by strong limitations on freedom. Only by arresting freedom of contract in this respect could monetary autonomy be preserved.

But of course things wouldn't stop there. For good reasons or bad—and I think some of the reasons, at least, are bad—national monetary authorities are not prepared to admit totally "clean" floating. We only have to remember the pother and flurry in 1971 when President Nixon declared the dollar inconvertible to remind ourselves of this tendency. And personally, I have yet to be convinced that "dirty" floating, which I regard as more or less inevitable, is likely to be accompanied by many fewer exchange controls than came into existence in various parts when it was attempted to maintain fixed parities.

Even that is not the end. Once you have installed limitations on free contract and extensive controls on exchange and capital movements, you have created, at least between the so-called key currencies, an oligopolistic situation in which no holds are barred—not only competitive depreciation but also all-out trade wars, with tariffs, quantitative restrictions, and so on. This hasn't happened yet on any very large scale. But a man would be out-Panglossing Pangloss who didn't recognize the present danger. If there are no supranational agreements, no restraints in the economic and financial sphere, then almost anything can happen.

So the matters we have to discuss at this fourth conference are matters of some practical urgency.

But how are we to discuss them? I am appalled by the task that you have assigned to me—especially in the terms in which you have defined it. Great experts are here assembled: and we have presiding over us the greatest expert in the chairmanship of conferences in the Western world, who will certainly know how to keep us in order and to arrange the detail of our deliberations. I may be forgiven, therefore, if I proceed in this introductory survey in a rather loose discursive manner, thinking aloud and touching very simply on broad issues which, in my judgment, ought to be at the back of our minds when we address ourselves later on to more technical problems. And I hope you will forgive me if at the outset I ascend to quite stratospheric heights and discuss one or two very pure hypothetical cases.

Assuming your agreement, let me therefore begin with a few remarks about the ideal gold standard, not—I repeat not— the gold standard as it has worked out in history and still lurks in the background of IMF regulations and of some, though not all, plans for reconstruction, but rather the gold standard of classical models: a state of affairs in which each national money is based on freely mintable, freely exportable gold coins or bars—represented, if you like, in internal circulation by credit instruments with, shall we say, 100 percent coverage. I need not recapitulate to an audience of experts the classical analysis of how such a system was supposed to work— the specie-flow mechanism, the great Ricardian Law of the Distribution of the Precious Metals.

Now, fellow delegates, we all know the popular argument against such a system—namely, that it puts the aggregate supply of money in the wide sense at the mercy of the vagaries of gold discovery and extractive techniques. We all learned this at the breast, so to speak, though I must say at this time of life that I am surprised at the number of people who still find it worthwhile to trot it out as though it were an astonishing discovery.

Moreover, it happens to be true. It is true that, under the gold standard so conceived, the stability of the value of money and of aggregate demand exists only by accident. And it is very easy indeed to think of discoveries of new ores or new techniques—or the absence of such discoveries—which would make it a matter of compulsory good sense to abolish such a system at once to avoid crass inflation or crass deflation.

Having said that, however, I can't resist the temptation to observe that, hitherto in world history, systems based upon metal have on the whole been much less unstable than other systems. The really great monetary catastrophes have been on paper, not metal; and although we may hope, as I most profoundly hope, that in the future we may do better, we must admit that up to date any success in this respect has been rather small.

But to come back to objections. I don't myself believe that the main criticism of the gold standard has sprung from any very profound worries about the empirical position in this aggregate respect. After all, if the tendencies to inflation or deflation which are at all likely in the world as we know it were to continue, it would be comparatively easy to deal with them. In this ideal classical model that I am talking about, given a reasonable degree of international agreement, something like Irving Fisher's Compensated Dollar—altering the weight of the unit of account to offset changes in its purchasing power—would certainly go some way to secure greater stability of the system.

Now surely, the underlying objection to this kind of standard is not nearly so much its aggregate instability as the fact that, if it is worked according to the rules, it brings it about that the various national moneys behave as if they were parts of a single system. In such a model, whatever is happening to the aggregate,. a relative expansion in one part is offset by a relative contraction elsewhere. I underline the word relative; for, of course, in a system of increasing money supply, the conditions of equilibrium don't necessarily involve an absolute contraction anywhere: they imply only a slower increase in one area than in another. But be that as it may, in certain conditions this offsetting process, which makes the whole behave as though it were one system, is apt to be resented and to give rise to policies which are destructive of the system.

Now what are these conditions? It is pretty clear that they do not arise within national boundaries. The ebb and flow of supply and demand may well give rise to prosperity in one part of a national area and depression in another; and we all know that this may give rise to all sorts of political commotions and suggestions. But it is seldom the case that we hear the complaint that the depressed areas are clamped into a common monetary system and that the appropriate cure would be to break it up. Only where the function of whatever governmental apparatus there may be includes responsibility for the independent manufacture of money—only there is this particular sort of suggestion likely to arise. Most of my working life I have listened to suggestions that the pound sterling should be freed from the tyranny of gold or the tyranny of a fixed parity with the dollar. Only once or twice have I heard it argued that the appropriate remedy for our depressed areas in Clydeside and the North East, for instance, would be to put them on a separate currency system.

If this analysis is correct, the fundamental objection to the classical gold-standard model is not so much that it rests on metal and all that, but rather that it is, as it were, the leading species of a larger conceptual genus: a common money between national areas. If we succeeded in devising a paper system more stable in value than gold, then I suggest in all seriousness that, so long as the world was divided into separate sovereign states with independent fiscal systems, then in the present state of public opinion there would be widespread objections to it.

Some of these objections, I fancy, would not be of a kind which would command much sympathy in this learned company. We shouldn't think it a strong objection to a common money <u>within</u> national boundaries that the city or county authorities were precluded from unlimited manufacture of currency or credit for financing independent and imprudent development schemes or for meeting inadmissable demands on the cost side. But some objections we should regard as more reasonable. We should at least understand the desire, in the absence of a common overriding international authority, to be in a position to produce more stability in local aggregate demand than would emerge spontaneously in the model I am criticizing. We might have great doubts about the success of such aspirations. But I submit that in the present state of opinion we should not regard them as perverse. And, indeed, surely this frame of mind is part of the problem of the world situation at the moment.

Let me turn to the opposite end of the intellectual spectrum that I am considering—to a state of affairs in which each sovereign state has a monetary system completely unconnected with any other. What would happen in such circumstances?

Well, I have said a bit about this already. I have suggested that, to preserve this complete independence, to preserve complete freedom of action, the various states would have to impose the most severe controls on transactions in moneys other than their own. Just as the gold clause in commercial contracts came to be prohibited in the monetary chaos of the 1930s, so dollar clauses, yen clauses, sterling clauses, and the like would have to be prohibited in regard to dealings between citizens of areas in which such moneys were not manufactured by the local states. To preserve the purity of the model that I am now considering, the whole Eurodollar market and its like would have to disappear. Because if local currencies fall into disuse owing to superior confidence in one or more foreign currencies, then the power of the local governments to manipulate their local economies would be reduced to a minimum. And in present conditions, that is something which few of them want, to put it very mildly.

But apart from that, there is a further consideration militating against the emergence of this model in all its purity. Whatever may be the intellectual arguments for clean floating all around, surely we know from grown-up experience that they are not going to be acted upon by quite a number of national authorities. If by some miraculous simultaneous conversion at a conference like this, all rates of exchange were to be freed overnight, few things can be more certain than that, within a few days, a great many of the smaller and weaker currency areas would have hitched themselves in one way or another to more important and stronger systems. The dollar area, the sterling area in the past, and similar arrangements came into being, not because they were imposed from above by international authority, but because of the spontaneous influence of obvious advantages to the inhabitants of the areas concerned.

Well, this could be elaborated very much further. But the main conclusion is surely pretty obvious. Although the world is organized into an absolutely ridiculous multiplicity of sovereign states, each aspiring to complete autonomy in the financial and commercial sphere, we are not likely to see, save at moments of extreme crisis, a complex of international monetary relations involving completely free markets for each national currency. However powerful the centrifugal forces militating against the creation of a completely common world money—my first model—the centripetal forces are also strong enough to impose a great deal of extranational consolidation or intermixture. I have taken a long time to reach this point. But I hope at least that I have made it clear that the concrete problem that this, or any other conference concerned with real problems, has to solve is the problem of the relationship, not between all currencies, but between key currencies.

Before saying a few words—and they won't be many—about this general problem, there is a special problem of what may be called a key area, on which I should like to make a few remarks. I refer to the problem of European monetary union.

At the outset, let me come quite clean. I am a definite "marketeer," to use the jargon of U. K. domestic controversy. I support the creation of a united Western Europe not, I hasten to say, because from my point of view this is the optimal conceivable association for our lifetime; for me that would be a united Western alliance—an Atlantic union with like-minded people from elsewhere included. I support it rather because, things having turned out as they have in the last twenty-five years, I think it is the best that we can get under present conditions. And I support it, let me add, not because of the economic benefits it may create—although, in spite of the absurdity of the agricultural system, I think that in the end these are probably not inconsiderable. I support it rather for basic political reasons. I think that if the nations of Western Europe cannot get together and create a viable political and military unit capable at least of defense in conventional warfare, they will be mopped up, one by one, by the Iron Curtain powers, as were the Grecian city states by Macedon and the Romans. And despite the slight detente in the world due to Mr. Nixon and Dr. Kissinger, I don't think the fundamental dangers are over. Indeed, I think the main danger to the free world is that so many people at present think they are.

That being my belief, I certainly think that a common money in this area is eventually desirable. Indeed, I can't believe that complete economic integration is possible without such an institution. I suspect that, even today, with the relatively small approach to a united Europe which is represented by the existing Common Market agreements, these arrangements are continually liable to be upset by the absence of monetary unity. I sympathize, therefore, with the attitude of those continental enthusiasts who stress the importance of this goal.

Nevertheless, with the best will in the world, I cannot persuade myself that a premature attempt to clamp the existing economies into a rigidly fixed common system would be anything but dangerous at this stage. We all know from bitter experience what damage can be done by the establishment of wrong parities; the restoration by Great Britain of the gold standard at a wrong parity in 1925 is of course the classic instance. And it is surely difficult to believe that the French economy would be in as good a state as it now is if, after the riots and wage increases of the late 1960s, it had not had some elbowroom for rate adjustment.

Moreover, given the present incomplete state of political unification in Western Europe, I personally don't think that the authorities of any one state would be justified in surrendering completely their powers of monetary autonomy while they are still liable to unaided military or quasi-military emergency. With no automatic response from associates absolutely guaranteed, it would surely be folly for them to abandon the means of raising the necessary finance for supporting such emergencies. Not until the European Economic Community approaches nearer to the form of a European Political and Defense Community will the use of a common money be either practicable or desirable.

In present circumstances, therefore, much as I personally desire the further unification of Western Europe—and it would not upset me to wake up one morning and find myself tricked into a complete federation—I incline to the view that, at the moment, some halfway house is the most we can hope for. This might well take the form of the old payments union, appropriately refurbished—clearing arrangements charged with powers to arrange adjustments of exchange rates where changes seem to be desirable, and holding certain reserves to facilitate such changes, if necessary. If at the same time a clearing union were to facilitate habits of drafting contracts in terms of some common tabular standard, some common unit of account, we might hope that it was helping to create the conditions in which greater eventual political unity would make possible the use of a common medium of exchange.

But Europe, as a key-currency area, is only part of the world, and the most outstanding problem is what is to be the relationship between key currencies in general: and that, doubtless, is the main question we have to discuss this weekend. As apparently I am to have the privilege on Sunday morning of some sort of general survey of the outcome, I restrict myself with underlining at this stage certain conspicuous issues.

I begin, not without trepidation, with the International Monetary Fund as an institution. As I have said before in this group and elsewhere, although one of the few surviving members of the conference at which this institution was brought to birth, I nowadays regret the cumbersome all-embracing constitution of that body, and I regret that at the beginning membership was not confined to the group of powers whose money really matters in international finance. Still, let me hasten to add, there it is, with a dedicated and supremely expert staff whose knowledge is a very positive asset to the world at large; and provided it comes to be taken for granted that the really important decisions are taken by a group which is small enough to permit a grown-up and secret conversation, I don't think it necessary to waste words discussing structural and constitutional changes which would take an unconscionable time to get through and cause quite a lot of purposeless recrimination in the meantime. The important questions relate not so much to constitution as to regulations regarding policy.

In this connection, the first problem relates to margins. I don't think this need detain us long. Assuming that there is not to be a free-for-all floating all around, about which I have already said all I want to say, I suspect that majority opinion nowadays inclines to considerably wider margins within which the various authorities are allowed to operate without reference back to the Fund. I myself accept this argument. I don't think such arrangements are ideal. But so long as there exists the possibility of agreed adjustments of the fundamental relationships—and so long as there exists no overriding political union and no single center of money manufacture—then surely adjustments from time to time may be necessary, and there ought to be margins for maneuver in which the central banks and their stabilization funds may operate with some success against embarrassing speculation.

As regards the fundamental adjustments, I am all for them as soon as there is reasonable evidence of underlying trends. And as a survivor from Bretton Woods, I would like to say that I don't admit that this is any departure from the spirit of that conference. It is subsequent practice rather than the spirit of the original statutes which has tended to undue rigidity, though I would like to add that, as regards U. S. practice at least, the underlying motive—the preservation of the value of balances deposited in the expectation of stability—was certainly not dishonorable and perhaps not quite so intellectually weak as it has sometimes been fashionable to argue.

But while I am all for speedy adjustment to underlying trends, I should be against the application of a mechanical formula. The fact seems to me to be that the influences giving rise to fundamental disequilibria in balances of payments, either positive or negative, are so various that it is difficult to think of any simple rule which would deal adequately with all cases. In particular—and I now become extremely controversial and provocative in this particular audience—I would urge that compulsion to <u>upward</u> valuations may occasionally be unjust. Needless to say—I hope it's needless to say—I can think of many cases when I should certainly recommend such adjustment in the interest of the area concerned. Favorable changes in the real terms of trade are an obvious instance, and I should also favor upward revaluation as a defense against inflations engendered elsewhere. But, especially in regard to the latter, I should argue that these were, in the present state of the world, essentially matters for the authorities concerned. To defend yourself against the imprudence of others is one thing; to be compelled to ease their position by adjustments which for local reasons you find inconvenient is quite another.

All this, however—the question of the width of margins, the question of fundamental adjustment—pales into insignificance before the question of the ultimate medium of international settlements, whether dollars, SDRs, or gold; and doubtless we shall spend a great part of our time discussing these alternatives.

In recent times, let's face it, the free world can be said— as dear Milton Friedman, always outspoken, has claimed—to be on a dollar standard. You can put all sorts of glosses on statements of that sort. Needless to say, the relationship between the dollar and other currencies can change. But although there has been a slight adjustment in the price at which the United States is not prepared to sell gold, the relationship with gold is supposed to be fixed. The dollar has not been regarded as free to fluctuate in the terms in which the IMF ultimately keeps its accounts—and the dollar is inconvertible.

Now this state of affairs surely is profoundly unsatisfactory. If the dollar were likely to be more stable in purchasing power than other currencies—and it must not be forgotten that, in spite of the recent crisis, the dollar has been more stable—it is difficult at this time of day to believe that the authorities of other key-currency areas can ultimately be content with a state of affairs which, at fixed rates, leaves the ultimate decisions concerning the value of money in the hands of the authorities of one area or, alternatively, throws the burden of adjustment always on their side.

This may be very wrongheaded. Certainly, the penumbra of anti-Americanism which so frequently accompanies discussions of this sort is something which I personally find quite contemptible. But in an atmosphere quite immune from this particular odor, I suspect that the mechanical facts that I am now discussing would ultimately still be unacceptable. And the fact that the dollar is not only a large constituent of the holdings of other systems but is also at the same time inconvertible renders the present situation even more unacceptable. I won't dwell here on the extreme fragility of the entire Eurodollar system, not to mention its uncontrollability, while this state of affairs persists. But it is quite clear, as we have seen in these last weeks, that the systems outside the United States are just not willing to accumulate indefinite masses of dollars, and—perhaps perversely, who shall say?—are unwilling that the onus of adjustment vis-a-vis a fixed weight of gold should always fall on them.

In such circumstances, it is natural, is it not, that the idea should emerge of using the International Monetary Fund as the keeper of the means of ultimate settlement, of using it to bring about conditions in which each key-currency country is able— in agreement, let us hope, with the others—to adjust its own rates in relation to the Fund's unit of account. This is a policy which must mean, in effect, turning the Fund into more of a bank—turning it into something much more like the Keynes Clearing Union than the plan which emerged from Bretton Woods. And as a means of bringing about this transmogrification, the instrument of special drawing rights, invented originally for another purpose, naturally comes to men's minds.

Well, I personally find much attraction in this conception, but subject to certain important provisos.

First—and I am now going to say something which I know will be very unpopular—I should regard it as undesirable for the allocation or issue of special drawing rights to be made an instrument of international charity—that is to say, of special privileges for the so-called underdeveloped areas. I hasten to say that I am not opposed to arrangements for helping these areas: I was in at the birth of the World Bank, and I'm not ashamed of it. But to extend assistance from the resources of the Fund on nonbanking grounds is the wrong way to help them; and I'm sure that to introduce this element into the work of the Fund, however transformed, would positively imperil its usefulness. The last thing that should be required of any sort of reserve bank is that it should get tied up on long-term or especially risky investment, directly or indirectly.

Second, I would insist that there should be built into the provision for the issue of these instruments strong safeguards against inflation—which certainly wasn't the case with the Keynes Clearing Union. The amount by which the aggregate of such issues should be allowed to increase should be subject to strict control. Now how this should be formulated—whether the control should consist of a Friedmanesque limiting percentage, only alterable by special voting devices, or whether there should be something more flexible but still immune from inflationary abuse—is a matter on which, I confess at the moment, I find it hard to make up my mind. But I am sure of this: that if the use of SDRs for this reason is to be an aid to the stabilization of financial relations in the free world, and not just another investment in the destruction which we see going on before our eyes, some limitation on inflation is an indispensable prerequisite.

This brings me to the last problem: the place of gold in such a system. I am not unaware that here at this conference I am surrounded by people I like very much, all consumed with the desire to see gold banished forever from the monetary system. I would like to assure them that I am really not unaware of the arguments in favor of this cause—I touched on some of them at the beginning of my remarks—and I can well believe that, in some future age less anxious than our own, with international relations organized on a more rational basis, there may take place a disappearance of the attitude which looks to gold as an ultimate safeguard against financial imprudence and against corporate and individual loss. But, fellow delegates, the fact is that at the present day, in many parts of the world, this frame of mind still persists, and it is surely burying our heads in the ground to ignore its existence. After all, as I pointed out at the beginning, we cannot claim yet awhile that national paper systems totally divorced from gold have had a particularly creditable record. Therefore, I do not think it foolish at this point of time to retain some arrangements whereby SDRs are convertible. At what price, and whether this price should be fixed or variable, are questions which it would be interesting to discuss later on. The point I am trying to make here is the probable desirability of some continuing link with gold, at any rate for some time.

I admit that gold may be a relic of barbarism. But it may also be a relic which prevents a relapse into conditions even more barbaric, in any true sense of the term, than those which in the present state of the world it is otherwise possible to achieve.

Well, be that as it may. I submit that even from the highly superficial survey I have given you, there are plenty of contro-

versial topics for discussion. To my way of thinking, there
are at least four which can be separately considered. First,
there is the problem of the future constitution and powers of
the International Monetary Fund. Second, there is the problem
of the rules and the mechanism of adjustment in the relations
between currencies. Third, there is the problem of the rules
of issue of SDRs. And finally, there is the problem of the
ultimate basis of the settlement system—whether gold, SDRs,
or perhaps something else. I am sure that there are many
more problems than these—for example, the control of capital
flows, repulsive as that subject is. But I hope I have said
enough to provoke discussion.

III. OFFICIAL PERSPECTIVES

Frank A. Southard, Jr.
Robert Solomon
Guenther Schleiminger

Among the members of the conference were three officials who were in a position to speak with authority about official thinking relating to international monetary reform: Frank A. Southard, Jr., Deputy Managing Director of the International Monetary Fund; Robert Solomon, Vice Chairman of the Deputies of the Committee of Twenty; and Guenther Schleiminger, the IMF Executive Director for Germany. It should be emphasized that the statements made by these members were presented, not as official views, but as background for a better understanding of international monetary issues.

R. H.

Chairman THORP: The Moderator has now put oil into our lamps, but those who go back to the days of kerosene lanterns know that it takes a little while for the oil to move up the wick to the point of illumination. Before we go any further, I think it is important that we acquire, firsthand, the information we need with respect to some of the monetary facts of life—particularly those that have emerged in recent weeks. Fortunately, we have with us Frank Southard, whose many years of experience as a top official at the International Monetary Fund place him in an unusually authoritative position to enlighten us. He has agreed to give us a brief summary of events as they appear from his vantage point. So Frank, will you take over?

FRANK A. SOUTHARD, JR.: Thank you, Willard. After the very good framework that Lord Robbins has laid out for us, I am not sure that there is very much need for me to add anything. But I will try to do in a few minutes what you have suggested—to talk briefly about the events of 1971-73, concentrating on the period from the Smithsonian settlement down to this past week.

I think everyone here is generally aware of what led up to the Smithsonian arrangements: the growing strength of the payments position of other industrial countries—especially Japan and Germany, but by no means only those countries—and relatively, therefore, the growing weakness of the U. S. payments position. Despite all U. S. efforts—despite the policy shifts and the defensive measures of encouragement to American trade—the U. S. payments position prior to 1971 did not strengthen as one might have hoped, and the dollar thus became a clear target for a confidence crisis. We all remember such recent history as the heavy gold payments the United States had to make in the late spring and summer of 1971. During that period, we had the first of what I would call "the billion-dollar days"—days in which, to our amazement and horror, we found that funds amounting to a billion dollars could move into a single country.

It was a very reluctant U. S. government that finally was pushed into the so-called August actions of 1971, and I need not to this audience describe those actions except to remind you that they were followed by a general floating of currencies against the dollar. We then had an awkward period of almost exactly four months between the August events of 1971 and the Smithsonian settlement of December. During that period, there was more than one computer exercise on the appropriate pattern of exchange rates that might be sought. The Monetary Fund worked one out that had actually been in the mill before the August events. It was supposed to be very secret, but it soon leaked to the press—a fact which did not increase the popularity of the Fund with the U. S. government. This computer exercise was not, in fact, much different from the final outcome of the Smithsonian settlement, and I think it is only fair that the record show that the U. S. experts, who had made their own calculations, regarded the Fund calculations as leading to an inadequate adjustment. It may be that history will show that the U. S. government was right.

There was also during this period of tense four months an insistence from several quarters, including the Fund (an insistence which again was not popular within the U. S. government), that the United States should make its contribution to whatever settlement finally emerged. This meant, to put the matter in simple terms, that the United States couldn't hope to sit at the zero point, with all adjustments taking place from the zero point. In other words, the United States would have to raise the price of gold. Well, despite the unhappiness of U. S. financial leadership with that prospect, it finally happened; and the settlement, as you all remember, was a mixture of downs and ups, with the U. S. dollar going down, the official price of gold going up about 8 percent, the yen going up much higher, the D-mark very definitely higher, sterling and the French franc staying put, and other currencies regrouping themselves around these variables.

Here again, it will probably be the testimony of history that those people in the United Kingdom who felt that the pound sterling really should not have stayed put alongside the French franc may turn out to have been right. It should be recalled, however, that the U. K. balance of payments had been very strong—surprisingly strong—reflecting apparently the full result of the November 1967 devaluation of sterling to $2.40. There had not yet been any evidence of the big worsening of the U. K. current account which was to come in 1972. If that had come earlier, one would, of course, have wondered whether there could really have been a justification for sterling to remain unchanged along with the stronger French franc. In any case, these two currencies became, in effect, the fulcrum of the up-and-down settlements, and it didn't look as if there were any other way out.

Leaving aside some U. S. regret, I think it is probably fair to say that the Smithsonian settlement was generally regarded as a pretty good and fairly adequate arrangement. It was expected by everyone that there would be lags. We knew from the experience of the United Kingdom and of India, to take two quite big economies, that there is a lag of something like two years before a change in the exchange rate works its way through the payments system. So there was a willingness to be patient. Everybody knew that the immediate results tend to be perverse, and the fact that in the early months they were perverse did not really upset informed observers very much.

But as 1972 moved on, many people—and certainly I was one of them—began to feel rather unhappy and disappointed at the outcome that was developing, quarter by quarter, in the U. S. balance of payments. It was also evident that, for various reasons, the 17 percent appreciation of the yen wasn't having very much effect. As for Germany—Mr. Schleiminger is here, and he certainly knows the facts much better than I do—I would say that during the first three quarters of 1972 there was probably a general feeling that the German payments position was swinging around pretty well; by the third quarter, the German current account was not unduly disturbing to anyone seeking a redressing of the payments positions of the leading countries. But by the end of the year, there was even in the case of Germany a rather unexpected shift toward a position of greater surplus. With the U. S. balance of payments showing no improvement whatever and with the dollar overhang actually increasing, the scene was not a good one. By the end of the year, anyone who was watching the situation could not help feeling that we were heading into a situation that could easily develop into another crisis.

Now whether this crisis needed to come when it did, whether another six months would have finally shown some better results, nobody will ever know. In any case, crises come when they come, and the events that led up to this recent crisis were fairly evident. There was, of course, the reversal in the U. K. payments position—a rather quick reversal, in which the pound by the middle of 1972 again became the target for speculation and, as we all remember, was allowed to float. I would say that, by and large, that probably was a justifiable action by the U. K. authorities. In addition, as I have said, there was some unexpected strength in the German position toward the end of the year. Then there was the Italian action, with Italy setting up a dual market for the lira. Whether the Italians were justified in this action is perhaps debatable. They were trying to do something to stop the steady outflow of funds that was taking place largely because of political uncertainties over a long period of time, but, recognizing that their current-account position was very strong, they very properly kept the commercial rate pegged.

Then the Swiss panicked. I think we have to use the word "panicked," because, after all, the worst day they had, if I recall correctly, involved an inflow of a little over $200 million, which is mere chicken feed in this business. But to everyone's amazement, they let the Swiss franc float, and this certainly didn't help matters. By this time, the wind was up again, and it was just a question of when it would hit hard and what the target would be.

There were two targets: the D-mark and the yen. The Japanese have a much tighter and more subtle system of controls than the Germans—Mr. Schleiminger, I am sure, would agree—and as a result, although there was a movement of funds into Japan, it probably did not go very much over $1 billion during a period of about ten days. But the German controls, such as they are, were not in any way capable of preventing funds from moving in through banking channels if the persons or institutions moving them in were indifferent to the fact that they would not be earning any interest or even might lose a little on the deal in the short run.

So at this time we had the first two-billion dollar day. I am not prepared to forecast whether we will ever get to a three-billion dollar day, since I had never thought we would get to a one-billion—much less a two-billion—dollar day. The total movement of funds into Germany in these very few days was something in excess of $6 billion, which Mr. Schleiminger told me is equivalent to about 20 percent of the German money supply. We can well imagine what this did to the sleep habits of Dr. Emminger and his colleagues in the German central bank who were worrying about what was going to happen to their monetary policy. Taking all countries into account, those few days must have involved about $10 billion of flow out of dollars into other currencies.

We all know the outcome of this crisis. One of its most interesting aspects is that, in contrast to the intense U. S. resistance to the first devaluation of December 1971, this time the United States was prepared to move promptly in the discussions that went on and to make its own proposal to devalue the dollar by 10 percent.

This is obviously an important new development. It does not mean, it seems to me, that the dollar can float; under existing arrangements, all other currencies can float, but the dollar can't. But at least the dollar parity can be changed, and it can be changed quickly. Within the Fund staff, the consensus was that, prior to the recent devaluation, the dollar was still overvalued and the yen was still undervalued. The yen, of course, is floating, and it has floated up probably rather more than the Japanese themselves might have figured—although the float is perhaps not all that "clean," to use the current lingo.

Will the new devaluation work? As I said yesterday in my talk at Pomona College, if it doesn't work, we are in for real trouble. Because then the question will be: What is to be the mechanism of adjustment? If this big a change in the pattern of exchange rates over the period 1971-73 won't produce a better balance, then, of course, we shall have to face a much more agonizing set of appraisals.

Chairman THORP: We have another source to draw on for additional factual background—a source which is at the very center of current planning in the field of international monetary reform. As we all know, such planning was discussed for a considerable period of time by a Committee of Ten; that committee has now expanded to twenty. Population growth is difficult to check; our present conference is larger than it has ever been before.

The Committee of Twenty has a group of deputies. Those of you who are familiar with government and with intergovernmental operations know that the best way to learn the answers about what is happening in any high-level committee is from the deputies, and we are fortunate indeed to have with us Robert Solomon, Vice Chairman of the Deputies of the Committee of Twenty. He has agreed to enlighten us, to the extent he believes is permissible, on the activities of the Committee of Twenty.

ROBERT SOLOMON: I shall try to give you one man's impression of where the Committee of Twenty stands. I won't be revealing anything very shocking or exciting, but I shall follow the procedure that our chairman, Jeremy Morse, has used in press conferences of not identifying particular national positions. Of course, where national positions have been made public, one can refer to them, and Lord Robbins has already done that. In this connection, I hope that my good friend, Guenther Schleiminger, will be given an opportunity to correct the many biases that I will undoubtedly inject into the remarks that you are about to hear.

With this introduction, let me say that the Committee of Deputies has thus far had two substantive meetings and, brilliant and efficient as the deputies are, one does not change the world in two meetings. Nevertheless, from what discussion there has been, plus what one knows from the IMF report on "Reform of the International Monetary System," plus what is publicly known about national positions, I can start by saying that there is broad agreement on a few propositions. Let me state those propositions first, and then let me become a little more detailed on where I think the Committee of Twenty stands on the two major areas of reform: the adjustment process, on the one hand, and the reserve-settlement system, on the other.

I think there is broad agreement that international monetary arrangements ought to be more symmetrical: more symmetrical in the sense that both surplus countries and deficit countries should feel the need to adjust, more symmetrical in the sense that the payments equilibrium of other countries should not depend upon the payments deficit of one country (namely, the United States), and more symmetrical in the sense that the United States should have the same rights and obligations to undertake adjustment action as other countries. Those rights apparently have been exercised by the United States in the crisis just past, as Frank Southard has reminded us. There is also a broad feeling that the settlement and reserve system ought to be more symmetrical—implying, for one thing, a system of convertibility or a form of asset settlement, as the term is used in the Fund report. Finally, although this has not yet been discussed in any detail in the Committee of Twenty, there is some feeling that the intervention system should be more symmetrical.

Now let me try to say a little bit more, still in an unexciting way, about where discussion has been moving in regard to the adjustment process. There is broad agreement that we need a strengthened consultation procedure if we are to have an improved adjustment process, and there has been much talk of so-called "objective indicators" or presumptive criteria to help guide a better adjustment process. The American proposal, which has recently been published as an appendix to the annual report of the Council of Economic Advisers, is based on using changes in reserves as an indicator of the need to adjust. The reasoning behind this proposal is that if we are to have a convertibility system, then it makes sense to regard changes in reserves as the indicator that guides adjustment. There has been much discussion on how indicators might be fitted into a strengthened consultation procedure. Three possible uses of indicators have been identified, and are being discussed.

First, an indicator might be used simply to trigger international consultation. If an indicator of balance-of-payments performance—whether it were a change in reserves, a change in the basic balance of payments, or a change in forward exchange rates—indicated that a country was moving toward imbalance in one direction or the other, that country would be called into the consultation process.

Without implying automaticity, a second possible use of indicators would be to trigger action—to identify the country or countries which might be taking policy action and to guide the actual taking of such action.

A third possible use of indicators would be to establish a presumption that the international community should put some form of pressure on countries that are in persistent imbalance. I am avoiding the word "sanction," which has unpleasant connotations from other fields, and I am using instead the word "pressure" to mean actions that the rest of the international community, through the Fund, might take to induce countries to act more vigorously and more promptly in correcting imbalances.

Of these three possible uses of indicators, the first—triggering consultation—has been discussed in the Committee of Twenty. There has been a beginning of discussion of the second possibility—triggering action—but there has been very little consideration thus far of the third possibility of graduated pressure that the international community might impose on countries which are in persistent imbalance. And I should go on to say that there is as yet no agreement on which indicator or indicators might be used for these various purposes.

Let me now make it clear that, in our discussions of the use of indicators, no one is talking about an automatic system. The American proposal is not a proposal for automaticity. A significant part of the press interpreted the American proposal as being one that called for an automatic response to changes in indicators and, since that was the initial interpretation, it became possible at a later stage for observers to come to the conclusion that the Americans had made a compromise by moving away from automaticity. Well, it is probably a good thing that people think the Americans are compromising, but it is not a question of automaticity; the issue with respect to indicators is just how compelling they should be regarded in any or all of the three uses I have identified in an improved adjustment process.

If indicators are to be used, but are not to be used automatically, it is obvious that we need some basis for deciding

when to overlook what the indicators are indicating. In any
event, even the strongest proponents of the use of indicators
in an improved adjustment process are fully aware that one
needs analysis, one needs forecasts, and one needs the sort
of detailed examination of payments positions that has been
carried on in the International Monetary Fund and in the Organization for Economic Cooperation and Development, particularly
in its Working Party III. At the same time, the consultation
that has gone on in the Fund and in the OECD during the past
clearly has not been sufficient. We might not be sitting here
today if there had been an adequate adjustment process. Everybody realizes that one has to go beyond simple consultation,
and it is that realization which has led to the discussion about
indicators that I have tried to describe to you.

Turning to the adjustment policies that might follow from the
consultation process I've just been talking about, I don't think
that any great new insights have emerged from the Committee
of Twenty discussions on the role of national policies. There
is a general recognition of the need for prompter changes in
exchange rates—not a very exciting observation. There is a
general belief that the device of temporary floating should be
legalized and brought under the surveillance of the International
Monetary Fund. That belief existed before last week; I assume
that it is even more widely held now.

Preliminary discussions have taken place on the use of
capital and trade controls in the adjustment process. The
general view is that these should not be relied upon as adjustment devices. I think there is general agreement that, where
there are restrictions on trade and other current-account
transactions, it is right that the removal of such restrictions
should be undertaken as an adjustment device by surplus countries, but there is opposition to the imposition of such restrictions as a means of dealing with payments deficits. With
regard to capital controls, the general feeling in the Committee
of Twenty is that these are less undesirable than trade restrictions, though the Committee has not yet examined the possible
role of capital controls in attempting to deal with destabilizing
short-term capital movements.

Let me now move on quickly to the second major area: the
reserve and settlement system. I shall have less to say about
this, because the Committee of Twenty has thus far spent less
time on the matter. I have already mentioned that there is
general agreement on a convertibility system—not a dollar

standard or any other single-currency standard but a system under which, generally speaking, imbalances would be financed by transfers of reserve assets rather than by changes in reserve liabilities. Since most other countries already finance their payments deficits with reserve assets, what this comes down to in practice is that the United States would also finance its deficits with reserve assets, and would receive reserve assets when it has payments surpluses. While there is, I think, general agreement on the desirability of a convertibility system, there is also a recognition that there needs to be some elasticity in that system. Whatever view one may have of the reserve-currency system as it has operated since Bretton Woods, that system did provide some elasticity—some would say too much. Nevertheless, any new system also needs some degree of elasticity.

Another matter on which there is broad agreement is that the SDR should become the major asset, as well as the "numeraire," of the system. The question of how many SDRs to create—a problem to which Lord Robbins referred—is under examination by the Committee and, as he told us quite rightly, it is not an easy question to answer. There is broad agreement that the volume of international reserves ought to be under international management and that the growth of reserves over time should come primarily from the creation of new SDRs.

I need hardly tell you that the Committee is keenly aware of the problem of the "overhang" of reserve currencies, and various forms of consolidation are being studied. Two broad types of possible action have been examined. The first would be the establishment of facilities, such as are described in the Fund report, for substituting SDRs for existing reserve-currency balances. In this connection, there is an Italian proposal which, I believe, has been made public by the Italian authorities and has received some attention. The other broad form of consolidation would be bilateral funding between reserve centers and the holders of reserve-currency balances. On these matters there is some divergence of opinion; in particular, one finds that a number of countries—they tend to be the developing countries but are not exclusively the developing countries—feel that they would like to have continued freedom to manage the composition of their own reserves. This is clearly an area where a little reconciliation is needed.

Last but perhaps not least, there is the question of what to do about gold in a reformed reserve system. This is a matter on which there is definitely not any broad agreement at present, and I raise the subject simply to identify one of the problems which must be solved.

Well that, Mr. Chairman, is a rather unsatisfactory summary of what the Committee of Twenty has done thus far. International monetary reform is a long and complex process. It is bound to be long and complex, not only because the Committee of Twenty happens to be a cumbersome group, but because the world is a cumbersome world. Reform means change. When I feel a bit cynical about the Committee of Twenty, it seems to me that everybody wants reform but nobody wants change. In any case, the technical problems alone would make reform a lengthy process, and we are all aware that by no means all of the problems are purely technical. So we should not be discouraged by the fact that we don't yet have a finished blueprint for the future and that it will take a while before we do.

I hope that Guenther Schleiminger will now remove any biases that have been reflected in my remarks.

Chairman THORP: It is easy to be discouraged when conflicting interests exist, but I am sure we all hope that the Committee has sufficient drive and focus to find a way through these problems. Our next speaker is Guenther Schleiminger, who represents Germany on the IMF Executive Board.

GUENTHER SCHLEIMINGER: Mr. Chairman, instead of removing biases, I would find it more challenging and interesting to introduce some of my own. I hope this procedure will be acceptable to you, because we have already received from Bob Solomon a very objective, accurate, fair, and balanced survey, as becomes the vice chairman of a negotiating body.

Throughout my career, I have had to defend the interests and viewpoints of actual or potential surplus countries. For this group of countries, the key issue of reform is how to achieve more effective control of international liquidity. It appears to us that in the late 1960s, which ended with the creation of SDRs, we really grabbed the wrong end of the Triffin dilemma. At that time, we prepared for a period of reserve stringency that we feared would result from an expected return to balance in the U. S. payments position. Now as Frank Southard made clear, the U. S. balance of payments has certainly not moved in this direction, though we may hope that as a result of the realignment of exchange rates it will do so now. Whatever happens, we have the legacy of SDRs, and the experts are now discussing what this new instrument can offer as a vehicle for more far-reaching and more thorough reform.

While the SDR was originally considered as a supplement to other forms of reserves, there is now a growing readiness to establish this new primary reserve asset as the centerpiece of the system by phasing out, or at least phasing down, gold and the reserve currencies. In our view, such a development could lead, inter alia, to a better control of reserve creation—a matter which, as I said, is at the top of our list so far as the reform agenda is concerned. As it was the reserve-currency element which exploded before the realignment, and as gold—particularly with the development of the present market-price arrangement—does not really recommend itself as a centerpiece of reform, the SDR offers itself rather readily for this role.

But—and there's always a but—it is difficult to ignore the recent trend of disillusionment about the future of SDRs, particularly in Europe but stretching as far as Singapore. The disillusionment stems from increasing doubts about whether the original concept of the SDR as a man-made reserve asset can actually satisfy global reserve needs without leading to either a deflationary or an inflationary trend. For the SDR to function in the manner intended would require the IMF to be transformed into a kind of world central bank, independent of national interferences and pressures, and there is a feeling that this is a utopian dream. The political haggling on the size of future allocations of SDRs is regarded by a great part of the financial community with increasing uneasiness, and this uneasiness is augmented by the fact that the interest of the less developed countries in international monetary reform is almost exclusively limited to the so-called "link," involving the tying of the SDR to development aid.

I need hardly say that these doubts are not minimized by the support which the link concept receives from the academic world, including some of the very distinguished experts present at this conference. This support is motivated by humanitarian and other noble considerations which are well understood, but it does not brighten the future of SDRs, for reasons which Lord Robbins has stated much more eloquently than I can. People have begun to wonder whether international reserve creation mainly through SDRs may not be an even more irrational process than reserve creation via the vagaries of gold production or via the payments deficits of reserve centers, since the decisions involving SDR creation would be subject to politicizing in the worst possible sense. I do not want to overemphasize this point, Mr. Chairman, because the alternatives to SDRs are not very attractive either, but, as Lord Robbins has already made the point, I would stress that his warnings should be taken seriously, because his fears are widely shared.

I now come to another matter which Bob Solomon mentioned— namely, the subject of international adjustment. As a representative of a surplus country, let me first say a few words about exchange-rate policy. We think it would be a mistake for countries to rely too heavily on exchange-rate adjustment as a solution for problems which are better handled by other means. We are still in an inflationary period. It would be extremely dangerous to remove the stoppers which force countries to pursue policies that keep them on an even keel. We believe that the major industrial countries still need to rely strongly on domestic adjustment measures in view of the increasing degree of international integration that has already occurred, not only within Europe, but also within the Atlantic community through the emergence of the Eurodollar market and through the expanding role of multinational corporations. Because of these developments, it would be a mistake, we feel, to rely too much on exchange-rate adjustment. Where exchange-rate changes are contemplated, we feel that objective criteria should have a place, but as a trigger for consultation rather than as a trigger for action. We would agree, of course, that consultation procedures should be geared in such a way that they lead to decision-making—in other words, that consultation should not be merely for consultation's sake.

Finally, a word about convertibility. In our view, convertibility is an indispensable condition for a multilateral and nondiscriminatory international trade and payments system. There are a number of plans on the table. It is not my intention to go into the detail of these plans, which will now be the subject of intensive study, but simply to indicate our own view that some form of convertibility is indispensable.

IV. INTERNATIONAL MONETARY REFORM: EXCHANGE-RATE ISSUES

*Robert A. Mundell and
Members of the Conference*

Chairman THORP: After listening to the various presentations this morning, it seems to me that the first issue we should discuss is what changes there should be in the exchange-rate mechanism in order to make it more effective and more conducive to economic well-being than it has been during the recent period of recurring crises. On this matter, a host of questions have been raised by our speakers already, so I propose that we devote this afternoon to considering them. Our first speaker will be Robert Mundell.

ROBERT A. MUNDELL: I am pleased that the Chairman has asked me to introduce the topic of exchange-rate policy. I have come to the view that the way in which exchange-rate changes affect balances of payments and levels of unemployment is quite different from what we were led to believe as a result of studies based on assumptions that were relevant, or appeared to be relevant, to the world of the 1930s. Models based on the assumption of infinite elasticity of supply in terms of domestic currency may have applied—though I'm prepared to doubt that— under conditions prevailing during the Great Depression. But such models are not relevant today. The standard conclusion that a devaluation is going to change basic long-run competitive conditions—that is, relative prices in the world economy—is valid only if money-wage rates expressed in terms of local currencies remain constant.

Now in a world of deflation, when prices are going down, I think Keynes was correct to adopt the premise that money-wage rates are constant within the relevant time period for employment analysis and that money illusion prevails in the very short run. But general inflation has invalidated this premise under present conditions, and money-wage rates may not only keep up with, but anticipate, inflationary trends. One implication of this is that classical rather than Keynesian conclusions hold in many areas of international economics. It means that we can no longer rely on a change in the exchange rate to improve the balance of trade through an alteration in relative prices.

I do not believe, for example, that if Canada were to halve the value of the Canadian dollar in relation to the U. S. dollar, this would improve the Canadian trade balance. Instead, it would simply cause a vast inflation in Canada, more or less doubling the Canadian price level as the money supply is forced to adjust, through central bank policy, to validate the new exchange rate. The same is true, I think, in nearly all countries—that large devaluations do not improve the balance of trade; they merely raise prices or replace price decreases that would have taken place had the devaluation not occurred. In the Keynesian model, this conclusion would have been admitted only as a long-run consequence. But, because of the speed-up of information, lag structures have now been reduced sufficiently to transform the long run into the short run.

An analogous conclusion holds for upward revaluations. The primary effect of currency appreciation is to reduce the rate of wage and price inflation in the appreciating countries. The effect of decreasing money illusion in such countries as Germany and Japan has made currency appreciation increasingly ineffective as an influence on the balance of trade and the level of employment.

I don't mean to say that changes in exchange rates don't change things, or that exchange rates don't matter. They change the rate of inflation. While it is true that a change in the terms of trade can alter the trade balance and the level of employment, it is no longer true that a change in the exchange rate can change the terms of trade. The terms of trade are determined by real forces, whereas exchange rates are monetary phenomena. If the Swiss franc is allowed to float upward by 2 or 3 or 4 percent a year, the effect of this exchange-rate change is to keep prices from going up in Switzerland as fast as they otherwise would, rather than to change the underlying real payments position. The same is true for the yen and the D-mark.

Chairman THORP: Lord Robbins has a question.

Lord ROBBINS: Before Bob finishes, I would like to ask him how he interprets the dramatic change in the British balance-of-payments position after the November 1967 devaluation.

MUNDELL: In my opinion, the major reason for the improvement following the 1967 devaluation was not the devaluation but the introduction of a new program of credit restraint. Devaluation can improve the balance of payments because it creates money scarcity and reduces absorption of the private sector, releasing goods for exports as the public saves more in order to rebuild liquidity positions—provided this is not offset by increased absorption by the public sector. One of the great successes of the International Monetary Fund after the U. K. devaluation was its achievement in persuading the U. K. monetary authorities to shift to a position of controlling the rate of credit expansion. Had the same credit restrictions been applied without devaluation, the balance of payments would have likewise improved—without the excessive price explosion that did in fact occur.

ISAIAH FRANK: I would like to ask Bob if he would apply what he has just said about the inflationary effects of devaluation to the experience of the United States, where trade plays such a small role in the total economy.

MUNDELL: Devaluation now is a treacherous word when applied to the U. S. dollar, because it can mean a rise in the nonoperative official price of gold, a change in the SDR parity, a change in exchange rates, or even a fall in the goods value of the dollar—which is itself a common definition of inflation.

With respect to the recent U. S. actions, we have to ask what exchange rates will be changed. If all other parities were adjusted with the dollar, no exchange rates would be altered, and the major impact of the devaluation would be on gold-guaranteed commitments of debtors to the IMF and on the price at which gold is allowed to be, but in fact is not, traded among central banks. Because the official price of gold will still be below its price in the private market, a devaluation of the dollar in terms of its gold and SDR parity that is matched by all other countries—leaving exchange rates between currencies unaltered—should not cause any significant change in world prices, unless, for unexplained reasons, it is taken as an excuse to increase national money supplies.

Because of the special role of the dollar as an international unit of account and the dominant size of its transactions area in the world economy, the effect of devaluation on inflation in the United States has to be given a different answer from that relating to a small country. A small country cannot change world prices much, so national prices have to change. In a small country, devaluation raises prices expressed in the national currency by virtually the full extent of the devaluation—over and above what would have occurred had the devaluation not taken place. This is obvious, of course, in the case of traded goods for which there is an international market, but the proposition holds equally, although with a longer time lag, for domestic goods, for the simple reason that the price relationship between traded goods and domestic goods is not in the long run altered by purely monetary changes.

But the United States is not a small country. The transactions area of the dollar covers over half the world economy. Even though traded goods represent only 5 percent of U. S. gross national product, U. S. trade exceeds that of any other country; and the dollar, despite inflation, persists as the dominant world unit of account. The effect of devaluation on U. S. prices, therefore, depends primarily on its impact on U. S. monetary policy and on the monetary policies of countries that devalue with the dollar. But because the dollar is inconvertible, the automaticity of the connection is broken. Thus I do not think that devaluation will have much effect on U. S. prices or on world dollar prices.

The February 1973 devaluation is an interesting political gesture, but the relevant economic change was the appreciation of other currencies relative to the dollar, which will alter inflation rates in the countries taking such action. If the United States changes the price at which it does not buy or sell gold, that is not going to change any prices unless it affects monetary policies or the pattern of exchange rates. What can change price levels is the degree to which the prices of the D-mark, the yen, and other currencies have gone up in relation to the dollar.

FRANK A. SOUTHARD, JR.: But the prices of many currencies have gone up.

MUNDELL: That is true. But whether they will stay up will depend on whether relative price relationships have arrived at a new equilibrium. If the exchange-rate changes have anticipated changes in the terms of trade made necessary by structural changes in demand and supply, they will be an alternative to price changes that would have occurred without them. But they do not correct trade balances. Indeed, I would not be surprised if the U. S. trade deficit should increase over the next four years. You can check this forecast at our next conference in Claremont! In any case, the U. S. trade deficit will tend to get increasingly more unfavorable if the United States moves toward becoming a mature creditor country.

Chairman THORP: Mr. Jamison has a question.

CONRAD C. JAMISON: My question is an expansion of the previous one. I would like Bob Mundell, if he would, to be a little more specific as to precisely how much of an inflationary impact he expects in the U. S. economy from the dollar devaluation of February 1973.

MUNDELL: Nil.

JOHN PARKE YOUNG: I would like to ask Bob about the devaluations of 1949, which covered a large part of the world and which were followed by a rather general improvement in the balances of payments of the countries concerned.

MUNDELL: The devaluations allowed the partial removal of exchange control, but did not result in trade surpluses. The United States had consistent surpluses in its trade balance during the 1950s. The British devalued in 1949 by 30 percent. Within a year and a half, they had a deficit in their real balance of trade, largely owing to the worsening of the terms of trade as a result of the Korean War boom in raw materials. But the main effect of sterling devaluation, I think, was to stimulate wage inflation in the British economy after 1949; on this matter, I tend to support Hawtrey's interpretation. Except for a brief period in 1954, the British were faced with systematic inflationary pressure and balance-of-payments deficits. Despite devaluation by the nondollar countries, a dollar shortage persisted in those countries that tried to neutralize the monetary effects of payments deficits.

Let me quickly illustrate the same point from the opposite side. In June 1970, Canada, in order to protect itself from U. S. inflation, let the Canadian dollar float upward in relation to the U. S. dollar. During that year, Canada had the lowest rate of inflation of any country in the world. After that, Canada continued to let the rate float, but, instead of a policy of monetary restraint, rapidly increased its money supply in order to prevent further appreciation of the Canadian dollar. As a result, Canada moved quickly to a position in which its rate of inflation was as high as that of any of the major OECD countries.

Here was a clear trade-off between currency appreciation and the rate of inflation. Of course, other factors were at work; I don't want to leave the impression that I am nothing more than a purchasing-power-parity theorist. But in a world where wide differences in monetary policy are taking place, it would be unwise for us to forget the purchasing-power-parity doctrine.

Chairman THORP: The Chairman, having in mind that there have been numerous devaluations in the past, will rule out any questions which ask Bob to explain how any of these devaluations support his theory. Mr. Silk has asked for the floor, and I trust that his question is of a broader character.

LEONARD S. SILK: I would like to ask Bob if he has now decided that exchange-rate flexibility is indeed a bad thing, breeding inflation as it goes.

MUNDELL: Whether exchange-rate flexibility is good or bad depends on the degree of money illusion in the system. If there is a large measure of money illusion, the old arguments for exchange-rate flexibility continue to hold and to have relevance. If there is zero money illusion in the system, these arguments have no relevance whatever.

SILK: Well, money illusion is one thing, but what about power? I may have no money illusion, but I have damned little power to adjust my money wage to what I would like my real wage to be. In any case, I thought you said that the effect of the U. S. devaluation on U. S. inflation would be zero, so how does money illusion get into the argument?

MUNDELL: Exchange-rate flexibility is an entirely different matter from U. S. devaluation in the form of a change in the official price of gold—a price that before and after the devaluation is inoperative. The really important changes in exchange rates have been the appreciation of the D-mark and the yen. I do not expect world prices to be much different because of the exchange-rate changes. I don't think that the price of chemicals, the price of cameras, the price of automobiles, and the price of a wide range of other goods will change very much in the United States. And I don't think the exchange-rate changes are going to have one iota of effect on the wage requirements of Mr. Meany's workers or of any of the trade unions in the United States. Do you?

SILK: No, I don't think the effect will be very large.

MUNDELL: Well, how large? The U. S. gross national product is in the neighborhood of $1.2 trillion. What effect is devaluation going to have on real wages in the United States?

SILK: One iota.

Chairman THORP: I suggest at this point that we appoint a subcommittee of Mr. Silk and Mr. Mundell to resolve this problem. Mr. Schleiminger has asked for the floor.

GUENTHER SCHLEIMINGER: Just one brief question for Professor Mundell: Would he recommend or tolerate exchange-rate changes as an anticyclical policy? We in Germany have been accused of abusing exchange-rate policy for just this purpose.

MUNDELL: Well, that's an internal problem within Germany. As I said before, I think the only reason for using exchange-rate changes now is to change the rate of inflation. If a country decides that it will not accept the world rate of inflation, then it has to let its exchange rate appreciate; and if a country is unsuccessful in keeping its rate of inflation down to the world rate, then it will have to let its exchange rate depreciate.

I don't think that exchange-rate changes will work any longer as an anticyclical device. There is no scope for a country like Britain, for example, with a million people unemployed, to devalue as a means of eliminating the unemployment. It won't work; it will just cause more inflation in Britain. In Canada, we have unemployment of 600,000 people. Canada could lower the exchange rate as much as it likes, but that would affect only the rate of inflation in Canada, not the level of unemployment. So I would say that, although the situation might have been different a decade or two ago, changes in exchange rates are no longer of much use as an anticyclical device.

Chairman THORP: Mr. Salant wants to ask a question.

WALTER S. SALANT: My question concerns the theory of money illusion. Bob Mundell surely exaggerates if his conclusion is that changes in exchange rates have no effect at all on the trade balance. The absence of any money illusion would seem to imply that the supply curve of labor in terms of money—this is putting the matter the way Bob did—would go up in proportion to the price level.

Now if a devaluation raises the price of foreign currencies by X percent, I would suppose that the price level would go up, not by the full X percent, but by some fraction of X percent, and, therefore—assuming no money illusion—that the wage level would go up by only this fraction of X percent as a result of devaluation. Consequently, it seems to me that the price-level change, even in the complete absence of money illusion, wouldn't cancel the whole thing. The absence of money illusion merely means, it seems to me, that you need more devaluation to get a given trade effect than you need when money illusion is present. I don't see how Bob can come to the conclusion that devaluation has no effect at all on the trade balance. I would be interested in hearing his reactions.

MUNDELL: Walter accepts the direction of what I said, but thinks I exaggerate my point because I fail to take into account his limiting case. My reply would be that his limiting case is not really a limit, because a 10 percent devaluation that led to the expectation of future devaluations and future increases in prices could induce wage increases of more than 10 percent. Money-wage rates might rise by 15 or 20 percent, in which case there would be a reduction rather than a gain in international competitiveness as a result of devaluation.

Now this is an empirical question, Walter, and I would suggest that we look at the actual results of recent devaluations. After seeing the failure of past devaluations, many people now take refuge in the argument that it takes three years for devaluation to work itself out. Where did this magic number come from? All I can conclude is that devaluation has been shown empirically not to affect trade balances the way people thought it did, so they invented a time horizon of three years and told us, in effect, that if we waited until that beautiful day three years from now, we would get a favorable delayed reaction. Well, there is no empirical foundation for that idea whatsoever.

Chairman THORP: Sir Roy, the floor is yours.

Sir ROY HARROD: Just a few words on the question raised by Bob Mundell—the effect of devaluation on the trade balance. That all depends on elasticities of supply and demand. Devaluation might go either way; it might worsen the trade balance or it might improve it. On the whole, recent experience does not suggest that devaluation usually results in an improvement. I do think that, after a substantial time lag, the 1967 devaluation of sterling—though this isn't certain—has been responsible for some of the improvement in the U. K. trade balance. But we never know for certain whether a given devaluation is going to improve matters or make matters even worse.

Now if the elasticities that we are talking about are too low, then I would suggest that there is an alternative—namely, import restrictions. Generally, at meetings of this kind, import restrictions are regarded as a great evil which must at all costs be avoided. In my view, import restrictions are a trivial evil compared with policies for holding down the growth of national income and that sort of thing. Such restrictions only cut off a few marginal benefits. But if import restrictions cease to be frowned upon—and I think they should be— they should be employed under a code of international good behavior. The rules should be such that if countries in deficit are allowed to increase their import restrictions as a means of getting out of deficit, then there should be a complementary rule that countries in surplus should be expected to reduce their import restrictions.

Of course, the trouble is that the surplus countries are in a power position. Countries in surplus are under no compulsion to take action, but the deficit countries are—they cannot continue being in deficit indefinitely. The United States was in deficit for a long time, but even the United States was unable to get away with it forever. Most deficit countries have to do something about the situation very quickly. But the surplus countries can sit back and say, "Well, our reserves are accumulating; how very nice, we like that." Thus we need international rules which direct surplus countries to reduce their import restrictions and which provide that, if the surplus countries do not comply, then deficit countries should be officially authorized to impose discriminatory restrictions on imports from the noncomplying countries.

Chairman THORP: I think that we should reserve a later portion of the conference for a consideration of these trade questions, so I suggest that discussion of Sir Roy's proposal should be deferred until that time. The next speaker is Professor Machlup.

FRITZ MACHLUP: Mr. Chairman, more than twenty years ago I coined the term "elasticity pessimism." At that time, I found there were two kinds: one that expected the effects of devaluation on the trade balance to be very small, the other that expected the effects to be perverse. This period of elasticity pessimism was followed in the literature by a more optimistic period, in which some of the earlier conclusions were challenged. But until this afternoon, I thought it had never been doubted by anyone that devaluation is sometimes needed to adjust to a preceding or ongoing price inflation, or that the net effect of devaluation may be small or nil if at the same time credit and government spending are further expanded so that the overvaluation of the currency which the devaluation is designed to remedy is soon restored. I was quite surprised when we were told this afternoon that in the British case it was not the devaluation but the credit restriction that worked and that the devaluation, therefore, was not really necessary.

Of course, credit restriction with devaluation is one thing; credit restriction without devaluation is another. What helped Britain was to have a combination of the two. This combination made economic sense.

I think that Bob Mundell is in error when he says that the elasticity optimists assume an infinite elasticity of supply of exportables. He apparently has in mind the well known Lerner formula, which was spelled out in Lerner's <u>Economics of Control</u> but was soon modified in the literature. The formula is useful for pedagogic purposes, but sheds little light on the economics of devaluation. The elasticity optimists I know do not assume that the supply of exportables is infinitely elastic.

My next comment concerns Mundell's use of the term "money illusion." That term has confused so many students over the years that I would really beg Bob and his colleagues to stop using the word illusion when there is no one who is having such an illusion. A trade union trying to get higher wages, whether prices have risen or not, is not under any illusion. It simply wants as much as it can get. To describe these matters as presence or absence of money illusion is to confuse the issue.

Now the theory that we have heard from Mundell is this: devaluations do not improve the trade balance; they merely lead to wage and price inflation. By the same token, currency appreciations do not lead to a reduction in the export surplus; they merely deflate stock prices and commodity prices. This theory implicitly assumes certain monetary and fiscal policies about which one should not be silent; it offends the good sense of the theorist to speak of the effect of an exchange-rate change and not say a word about the accompanying fiscal and monetary policies.

MUNDELL: If I am to abandon the term "money illusion," I would like to urge Fritz Machlup to abandon the term "elasticity pessimism." In order to talk about elasticity pessimism, you have to talk about changes in relative prices, and my argument is based on the difficulty, or even impossibility, of changing relative prices.

PETER B. KENEN: I would like to make one or two comments on Bob Mundell's rather iconoclastic position concerning exchange rates.

Let me say right away that I agree with one observation Bob made—namely, that this most recent change in the U. S. par value may prove to be a system-shaking way of effecting the revaluation of a small number of currencies—those of countries where national rates of inflation and national rates of growth in productivity have been out of line with global averages. It may prove to be an awkward way of getting at what is admittedly an intractable yet narrowly focused problem for the system.

Bob's analysis of the effects of devaluation, though, leaves me just a bit puzzled. If I understand his response to Fritz Machlup, he is not asserting that demand elasticities are low. I did hear him suggest that supply elasticities may be low. I also heard him suggest—and I think that this is what Fritz Machlup was implying—that the obstacle to a successful devaluation is not a law of nature regulating the behavior of price levels but a law of predictable mischief on the part of governments. Governments are averse to following the policies that should go with exchange-rate adjustment. And a floating rate or a crawling-peg system only complicates the problem.

But here I'm puzzled. If Bob is saying—as I think I heard him say—that the principal effect of an exchange-rate change is to accelerate inflation in the devaluing country and to diminish inflation in the revaluing country, he is perhaps suggesting a very effective exchange-rate policy—to do the opposite of what is normally suggested. His analysis prescribes currency appreciation for the _deficit_ country in order to reduce the rate of inflation and improve the balance of payments. If I have misinterpreted Bob, I would like to know what he was really saying.

One more observation along the same lines. Bob said a few minutes ago that the United States would have to run a larger and larger import surplus in the future in order to accommodate the expanding income from U. S. investments abroad. The United States, in other words, will have to become a mature creditor country. I don't necessarily disagree with that conclusion, but I am curious to know what mechanism Bob would invoke to generate that surplus. How would he accomplish the change in relative prices necessary to achieve the change in the U. S. trade balance? Is there some device in Bob's rather pessimistic view of the world which will do the job?

My last observation has to do with empirical work on devaluation. I'm a bit sensitive on this point. I would submit, most respectfully, that careful empirical studies give ample reason to believe that the effects of devaluation do not unfold immediately—that it is not foolish to speak of a lag of two, three, or four years. We know that it often takes that long to deliver goods after they are ordered. The response of purchasers to changes in price cannot, then, be fully reflected in the trade balance, except to the extent that advance payments or progress payments are made before delivery. I am talking about almost all capital goods which are produced to order, not only complicated machinery. My argument applies even to such things as oil pipeline and to many other products that are ordered long in advance. It even applies, to some extent, to orders of consumer goods, since these are often ordered in bulk on long-term contract, and reordering takes place at intervals. I am not asserting, Bob, that after three years everything will be all right; I am merely saying that it would be wrong to expect the full effect of devaluation in much less than two or three years when one has in mind a country whose trade is largely in manufactured goods.

I do think that, whatever one's views on this subject, there is one major issue on the table before us. Can we design an effective international monetary system if governments behave in a mischievous fashion and fail to pursue appropriate domestic and international policies? I would be terribly concerned if we were to design a monetary system that assumes the best governmental conduct, not the worst.

Chairman THORP: The Chairman rules that Professor Kenen's statement consists largely of rhetorical questions which at the moment do not require answers.

MUNDELL: May I have thirty seconds?

Chairman THORP: Yes, but not a revalued thirty seconds. You may have thirty unrevalued seconds, and that's all.

MUNDELL: I would like to make a brief comment on Peter Kenen's remarks about the appropriate exchange-rate policy for a country with inflation. A deficit country which is suffering from inflationary pressure should follow a policy of monetary restriction to prevent its currency from depreciating. It should then let its currency appreciate if it is prepared to inflate at a lower rate than the world norm. But the appreciation should come as a consequence of the monetary restriction.

Chairman THORP: Gottfried, the floor is yours.

GOTTFRIED HABERLER: I would like to approach a somewhat different problem, though I will not be able to avoid touching on some of the matters just discussed. It seems to me that there is one obvious conclusion which we can draw from this last crisis and from the background that Frank Southard and Bob Solomon have given us. The lesson is that if the Japanese and Germans had followed the Swiss example of letting their currencies float upward, the crisis could have been cut short. The Germans would not have accumulated $6 billion, and they would be in a much better position today. I find their policies a little hard to understand. First, they refuse to float, then they buy $6 billion at the old exchange rate, and now, because of the February dollar devaluation, they have lost 10 percent on those dollars and on the dollars they already held.

Now you might say that the American policy of devaluing the dollar has saved the face of all sorts of people, and has brought about more exchange-rate changes than an upward float of the mark and the yen would have brought about. But I don't think this is really true, because when the mark goes up, as it has in the end, the neighboring surplus countries go along. They have learned their lesson. The Dutch knew it all along; when the Germans appreciate, they have to go along or they get a great deal of inflation. It has taken the Swiss and the Austrians a little longer to learn this lesson, but they learned it after 1969 when Germany appreciated and they failed to go along. So the exchange-rate pattern which would have come about if the Germans and the Japanese had floated would have been about the same as it is now. Germany would have saved a few billion marks, but if it prefers to lose a few billion marks rather than to lose face, that is its business.

Now let me say a few words about the matter of indicators for appropriate exchange-rate action. Any kind of indicator, I think, would have prescribed currency appreciation for the Germans and the Japanese. I do not mean that appreciation would have affected the trade balance very quickly. The recent appreciation of the mark and the yen will not change the German or the Japanese trade balance overnight, but I would have thought that appreciation is clearly a step in the right direction—though that is now questioned by this new pessimism we have just heard about this afternoon.

Of course, there are superficial empirical reasons for this pessimism. The United States had a tremendous deficit in 1972 despite the Smithsonian realignment and despite the fact that it had a lower rate of inflation than Germany, Japan, or almost anybody else. Art Laffer had an interesting article last week in the Wall Street Journal, in which he explained the change in the American trade balance last year—quite rightly, I think—in terms of what he called financial growth rates. I would prefer to use the term "differential cyclical experience." The United States had a very rapid expansion last year, whereas the Germans and the Japanese had a slowdown. A situation of this kind always produces a very large deficit for the United States, so there is no good reason to assume that exchange rates were not moving in the right direction.

It is also clear that the favorable effects of any devaluation can be dissipated if the country goes on inflating, but let me call your attention to the experience of some of the less developed countries. Take Brazil, which until recently had an inflation rate of around 20 percent a year. Every five or six weeks, the cruzeiro is depreciated by 1 or 2 percent. Can anyone deny that if Brazil did not continually depreciate, it would run into tremendous difficulty, or that the depreciation tends to bring about the correct change in the balance of payments? I find it impossible to deny that.

Let me turn to the question of whether the surplus countries or the deficit countries should do the adjusting. This matter is now being widely discussed, and I am sure that the Committee of Twenty will devote much study to it. One of the asymmetrical features of our present system is that there is more pressure to adjust on deficit countries than on surplus countries, because when a country runs out of reserves, it has to do something, whereas a country gaining reserves doesn't have to do anything. But I suggest that this asymmetry is not all that bad for the very simple reason that if a surplus country refuses to adjust, that country at least does not restrict trade. What a surplus country may do is to restrict capital inflows; I would not call this a good policy, but it is not very destructive of trade.

Let me conclude by calling attention to a fact which makes me optimistic despite the recent crises—namely, the simple fact that throughout the postwar years the volume of world trade has grown without interruption. The various currency crises not only have not interrupted—they have not even slowed down—the steady growth of international trade. This suggests to me that these crises, which are very spectacular and give rise to conferences such as this, are not as destructive as many would have us think. What are the terrible things which could happen? In the 1930s, there were terrible things. World trade shrank by more than half. Nothing like that has happened since World War II.

Why not? The main reason, I think, is that there has been no serious depression in any major country. Nor, with our present knowledge, is a serious depression likely in the future. A second reason is that, by and large, adjustment has been brought about by exchange-rate changes. These have sometimes come too late, but in the end they came; the deficit countries did not hold out indefinitely as they did in the 1930s. I don't say that the present system can't be improved, but I think it is not quite as bad as is often pictured.

Chairman THORP: The Chairman is concerned about this trend toward optimism. Can it be that exchange rates are no longer important, and that crises aren't really disturbing? I hope that Henry Wallich will unearth some remaining problem that we ought to consider.

HENRY C. WALLICH: I would first like to pay my respects to Bob Mundell. He asserts that real wages cannot be cut, going one step beyond Keynes, who said that money wages can't be cut; and Bob also asserts that governments always accommodate this insistence on uncut real wages. If we take the alternative hypothesis of Fritz Machlup, that government is capable of controlling the money supply, then it is clear that if government does not accommodate the higher money wages required to maintain constant real wages following devaluation, there will be unemployment, and the balance of payments will adjust via the income mechanism instead of via the price mechanism. So adjustment there will be if there is control over the money supply. But Bob may be right in implying that, for political reasons, such control is unlikely to be adequately exercised.

What I really want to say is that, after the events of last week, we are now very close to a flexible-rate system. The readiness of the United States to change the dollar parity has reduced the credibility of any fixed rate, and it will now take only very slight disequilibrium to produce massive speculation and further rate changes. I dislike this system. I think a flexible-rate system is not the wave of the future, but, at 6 percent rates of inflation, it is rather hopeless to plan on permanently fixed rates. So what we have to do now is to learn to live with, and manage, a system of flexible rates.

In this connection, I would like to make one or two suggestions. We know that prices tend to be sticky downwards, and not upwards. Exchange rates tend to be sticky upwards; as we have seen recently, countries are more willing to depreciate than to appreciate. Consequently, flexible exchange rates give rise to arguments along "Phillips-curve" lines. That is to say, we will be hearing a great deal about how we can reduce unemployment by accepting slightly higher rates of currency depreciation, ignoring the problems created for other countries. Since I share the views that have been expressed here about the disappearance of money illusion or what we might now call exchange-rate illusion, I don't think such techniques would work, and we ought to be on our guard against them.

Now what are the conditions under which flexible rates are likely to work well? It seems to me that long-run trends, such as in the rate of productivity growth, can easily be accommodated by flexible rates. Where we are going to have trouble is in short-run cyclical fluctuations, especially in cases of out-of-phase behavior of particular countries. A country that has a recession is likely to resort to competitive depreciation. A country that has inflation is likely to resort to tight money and thereby to appreciate its exchange rate. These are situations that will be very disturbing to the international monetary system, leading to controls and, despite what Gottfried has said, possibly even to a decline in trade.

What do we need therefore? Clearly, we need more control over cyclical conditions. We want this, of course, for domestic reasons, but we also need it if a flexible-rate system is to work satisfactorily. We will probably need coordination of monetary policies in order to prevent unstabilizing capital flows that would affect exchange rates. We will need incomes policies, as Sir Roy recommended in Bologna, and I would add that many countries do not have adequate instruments of monetary control. I think there ought to be a real push to make sure that all countries equip themselves with the kinds of defensive and equilibrating mechanisms that can decently be used, including negative interest rates and non-harmful control of capital movements, if there is such a thing.

Finally, let me turn to the possibility that we can salvage something like a system of fixed rates. It must be a system where rates can be changed very readily. I have proposed elsewhere a system in which the International Monetary Fund is authorized to change parities within limits that are set by the member countries. Countries would set these limits, not in terms of conventional parities, but in terms of the effective exchange rate. The system would operate in such a way that when a given change in the exchange rate pushed another currency outside the designated range of effective rates, the Fund would be required, when it changed the parity of country A, to make an appropriate change in the parity of country B. This would protect countries against rate changes by other countries that they could not live with. From time to time, the system would require another kind of Smithsonian arrangement in which countries would revise the ranges within which they were willing to have their effective exchange rates changed. If that were done, we would have, I think, a livable system of fixed rates.

Chairman THORP: I might remind you, Henry, that the Smithsonian Museum is where we keep our great national relics. Our next speaker is Professor Scitovsky.

TIBOR SCITOVSKY: Mr. Chairman, I have been one of the people who for years has been pleading for symmetry in adjustment. The history of the last few years gives the superficial impression that we have reached some degree of symmetry in the sense that surplus countries have been more eager than in the past to eliminate their surpluses and, in some cases, have revalued their currencies upward for this purpose. But I would like to point out that the analysis provided by Bob Mundell this afternoon indicates that there is another very different kind of asymmetry which still remains with us and which, I think, should be brought out into the open.

What I have in mind is this—that deficit countries, in wishing to eliminate their deficits, have a very different aim in view than surplus countries that are trying to eliminate their surpluses. Deficit countries want to stop their loss of reserves; surplus countries want to combat their inflationary pressures. Now it is much easier for the surplus country to achieve its aim. Appreciating the currency is all it has to do. But a deficit country which is trying to stop an outflow of reserves has to do more than devalue. The devaluation has to be accompanied by restrictive fiscal and monetary policies if it is to be effective. So here is a different kind of asymmetry: a surplus country only has to appreciate, whereas a deficit country has to do quite a bit beyond mere devaluation.

Chairman THORP: Professor Laffer has the floor.

ARTHUR B. LAFFER: My remarks are concerned with the economics of devaluation.

First, let me comment on Peter Kenen's point about lags in payment of two to four years. As time passes after a devaluation, we should expect to see more and more commodities coming into the payments cycle. This is a point that has often been made in the literature on elasticities—that the longer the time after devaluation, the greater are the elasticities. But if we look at the devaluations of the postwar period, we don't find a marked improvement in the trade balance as time goes on. I have looked at fifteen devaluations in the years since 1950, and for seven of those fifteen, the largest trade deficit, expressed in domestic currency, occurred three years after the year of devaluation. Incidentally, this was the largest trade deficit not only of the three years following devaluation but of the three years preceding devaluation. If there were an increase in elasticities as time went on, we should expect a gradual improvement in the trade balance after devaluation, but that is not what typically happens—at least in my cursory survey.

In our discussions thus far, we have not always distinguished unambiguously between the balance of trade and the overall balance of payments. After the devaluation of 1967, the British balance of payments appears to have improved substantially, even though the trade deficit, as measured in sterling, was larger in the three years after devaluation than in the two years preceding devaluation. When we look at devaluation and trade balances in a gross sense, the evidence does not lead strongly—or even weakly—to the conclusion that trade balances are greatly improved after devaluation. One of the problems, of course, is isolating the effect of devaluation from the effects of other policies concurrently pursued. Countries clearly can pursue fiscal, monetary, and commercial policies which either reinforce or neutralize the effect of devaluation—as when devaluation is followed by an increase in the money supply.

One final point. I would support the view that the deterioration in the U. S. trade balance has been a major boon to the U. S. economy. It has reduced excessive demand pressures in the United States.

Chairman THORP: One minute to Fritz Machlup.

MACHLUP: Art Laffer tells us that, according to his statistical investigations, there have been many devaluations which have not improved the trade balance. Of course there have, and nobody should be surprised, because in most cases devaluation is resorted to in order to adjust for a preceding period of demand inflation. In such cases, devaluation serves, not to improve the trade balance, but to prevent it from deteriorating further. In a good many other cases, the trade balance may not improve after a devaluation because devaluation is to serve only as a substitute for direct controls on payments. In such instances, increases in imports previously prevented by direct controls are prevented instead by higher prices for importables—or increases in exports as a result of devaluation are allowed to be compensated by increases in imports. Far from indicating that devaluation is a failure under such conditions, this outcome clearly reveals that devaluation is a success.

Chairman THORP: Mr. Southard has asked for the floor.

SOUTHARD: I can be very brief, Mr. Chairman, because I don't want to take the time of this group to pursue much further the analysis that Bob Mundell and Art Laffer have offered. I find myself having some of the same worries that they have expressed. So far as the United States is concerned, it seems to me that we may be heading into a period in which there are structural changes, particularly on the import side, which indicate that the mechanism of adjustment is going to be increasingly sluggish. I am thinking here of possible decreases in demand elasticities, and I mention fuel as only one of the possibilities. So we may be in for some very real problems.

But I hope that the Laffer-Mundell analysis doesn't get generalized to the whole range of countries of all sizes that have resorted to exchange-rate adjustment. And I would like to add that, in judging the effectiveness of devaluation, one must take into account the entire mix of policies concurrently pursued. It is certainly standard doctrine in the Fund that it is rarely of any use for a country to do nothing other than change the exchange rate. A successful devaluation, for example, requires an appropriate mix of domestic policies along with the exchange-rate change, and those domestic policies, at least in the smaller countries, need to be quite precise. But subject to this qualification, there has been a considerable number of what I would think must fairly be termed quite dramatic successes, where countries resorting to exchange-rate changes have been able to swing their balances of payments around, and where the process of adjustment has proceeded in quite orthodox ways.

Chairman THORP: Professor Cooper, one of our Yale delegation, has asked to make a statement.

RICHARD N. COOPER: I would like to make two sets of observations—one on the discussion started by Bob Mundell and the other on some matters which were raised this morning.

Bob has painted an exceedingly pessimistic view of how national economies work today. If you take his view literally, money illusion has reached the point—namely, zero—where changes in relative prices brought about by exchange-rate changes are very quickly washed out by corresponding adjustments in wages and other factor incomes.

This raises the question of what happens when other changes in relative prices take place in modern economies. For example, land rents rise continuously as populations grow, and fuel prices are also likely to rise relative to other prices. If it is indeed true that real wages are fixed, we are in the soup; necessary changes in relative prices cannot occur. This is not merely a question of exchange rates and their manipulation—that becomes a quite secondary issue. The fact is that modern mixed economies simply cannot function without changes in relative prices. And if the factors of production cannot tolerate any changes in real income, then we have insoluble problems.

I think that a realistic view of the situation suggests that the world is not in this bad a state—that, indeed, factors of production can and do accept changes in real income, including those brought about by changes in exchange rates.

This brings me to a second point. When exchange rates are fixed in a situation where countries have different rates of inflation, a change in relative prices will result. Within a country that is inflating more rapidly than the rest of the world, the prices of nontradable goods will rise in relation to the prices of tradable goods, the latter prices being determined by world market prices and by the fixed exchange rate. The purpose of devaluation in these circumstances is simply to restore the initial set of relative prices.

So a Mundell view of the world poses the question: What is the relevant starting point? Is it the disequilibrium set of relative prices that arose because one economy inflated more than the rest of the world under a regime of fixed exchange rates? Or is it the original equilibrium set of prices? Well, that's an empirical question. One can find cases, I am sure, in which some factors of production become so accustomed to the unsustainably high real incomes produced by a disequilibrium set of prices that they will indeed resist a change in relative prices brought about by devaluation. But Bob's comments cast a negative view on changes in exchange rates that is not warranted. Bob was implicitly arguing that if you have—however you got there—a set of disequilibrium relative prices, you can never get out of it through changes in exchange rates.

On another point, Mundell argues that devaluations and revaluations simply affect relative inflation rates. I would say that this is precisely what one wants to happen. The argument for a system of gliding parities, for example, is to compensate for divergent national trends in money wages and prices. Consequently, if one postulates starting out with an equilibrium set of relative prices which divergent national inflationary trends would disturb, then a gliding exchange rate is exactly the right mechanism to preserve over time the relative price relations with which the system began. Thus, using this line of reasoning, I would argue that changes in exchange rates, far from being damaging, are necessary so long as there are divergent trends in national price levels.

I would like now to shift the conversation to what was said this morning in somewhat different ways both by Lord Robbins and by Mr. Schleiminger. Each in his own way said that there should be no obligatory upward changes in exchange rates in the context of improvements in the adjustment process.

Schleiminger's version was that any objective indicators should signal, not action, but discussion, and Lord Robbins said that currency appreciation should not be obligatory. Yet it is in the nature of the situation that there will be obligatory devaluations, because when countries in deficit run out of reserves, they have to do something. Sooner or later, this usually ends up in the form of devaluation. Thus there is a kind of asymmetry implicit in the observations of both speakers.

Each of these two speakers in his own way also said that the present dollar standard is totally unacceptable and that it is necessary to have some form of convertibility—that, whatever role the dollar might ultimately play in the international monetary system, it would have to be a convertible dollar.

The combination of these two conditions implies either that the United States keys its domestic economic policy to balance-of-payments considerations—which I would argue is unwise not only from the point of view of the United States but also undesirable from the point of view of the world economy—or that the dollar, which is still the world's leading currency, will have to be devalued or depreciated whenever the United States runs into payments difficulties for whatever reason, including large surpluses confined to a single country. I would suggest that the combination of these stipulations introduces two capricious elements into the monetary system which it would be desirable to avoid.

The first is the unsettling effect arising from most countries having to decide just how much to adjust the values of their currencies following a devaluation of the dollar—a process that in general, and without coordination, will have to go through several interactions before the correct new set of rates is found. The second is the much less important but nevertheless similarly unsettling effect of frequent changes in the local-currency and international value of dollars held in official reserves if the dollar is depreciated even when the relationship between the United States and most other countries is in satisfactory balance. Both of these effects could be avoided under a system requiring upward changes in exchange rates when they minimize disturbance to the world economy.

MUNDELL: Since Dick Cooper has parodied my position, I would like to make it clear that no one should think that his interpretation of what I said has anything to do with what I was saying or with anything I have said in the past forty years.

Chairman THORP: Well, let's move on. Mr. Silk:

SILK: My comment follows from something said a little while ago by Sir Roy. I think there is a tendency for economists to regard adjustment, in itself, as a good thing and, in this connection, to become a little lyrical about the virtues of flexible exchange rates. Now we don't have that tendency for other kinds of prices. We don't celebrate if the price of IBM falls from 453 to 325 and say, "Great, we've had an adjustment!" I think this is something more than a truism, because there is danger in hailing exchange-rate flexibility as some kind of wonderful victory which exempts us from other kinds of concerns. And I detect precisely this tendency in the U. S. Administration—a feeling that, after all, what does it matter? If we have inflation, if we drop an incomes policy, if we adopt protectionist measures, or if we do anything else, the exchange rate will take care of things. That seems to me a very silly and false kind of euphoria.

I'm not arguing that fixed exchange rates automatically provide discipline against all kinds of evil. Obviously, they did not provide such discipline; if they had, the system would not have got into so much trouble. I do think that exchange rates need to adjust, but changes in exchange rates do not in themselves eliminate the need for appropriate action in the fiscal, monetary, and other fields.

ROBERT W. CLOWER: Most of the conversation this afternoon has impressed me as a surface battle about matters that don't really have a great deal to do with the basic problems of international monetary reform. Discussions of flexible and inflexible exchange rates and of the degree to which there is elasticity or inelasticity in supply and demand are interesting, but it strikes me that almost all of the problems that are really important here have to do with the degree to which a nation intervenes directly either to protect the interests of its own citizens against citizens abroad or to protect particular interests within the country from other interests within the same country.

With the gradual emergence of managed currencies and the absence of any automatic market discipline, the international discrimination that used to appear in the form of tariffs now appears in the form of devaluations, which in effect are like increases in tariffs, but they don't look quite the same. Of course, one may decide to combine exchange-rate flexibility with some form of trade restriction. The United States currently is bludgeoning various countries with the threat of direct controls if they don't accede to some kind of market controls. This approach is not very promising if its object is to get a hundred or more different central monetary authorities to cooperate.

I would be very interested to see what would happen if we recognized that in the foreign-exchange market we are dealing with something in which there is, in principle, a very strong hedging interest—what would happen if we allowed futures markets to develop fairly and freely, operating under rules that made price movements over any given day or week fairly orderly. I am sure that, in those circumstances, we would have a lot less trouble with so-called monetary crises. Under such conditions, the real burden of argument for protecting particular interests would be out in the open. I think we would be in a better position to deal with those arguments. As it is, we have a mixture of intervention at the direct level which is partly cloaked under the argument that we really can't handle the international monetary system.

SEYMOUR E. HARRIS: In 1936 I published a book called Exchange Depreciation, which was very much under the influence of Lord Keynes. During the 1930s, as we all know, there were many instances of devaluation and currency depreciation. Unfortunately, they didn't work out well, probably because, as Sir Roy Harrod would say, the fiscal and monetary policies were not well designed to deal with the widespread massive unemployment. Today, of course, our situation is entirely different from the situation prevailing in the 1930s. In the 1930s, every argument could be used for improving the general situation by increasing the supply of money. At the present time, such action would be inappropriate because of world inflation. I am not very hopeful that we are going to get out of our difficulties very easily even if Mr. Volcker, who is not known as a great optimist, says that all will be well in two years. In this case, I think he's being quite optimistic.

JAGDISH BHAGWATI: I would like to begin with a few remarks on Bob Mundell's thesis about the efficiency of exchange-rate changes. I'm a little worried, because nearly everybody who commented on Bob's views was accused by Bob of having misunderstood him, so I am not quite sure exactly what Bob will do to me. In any case, let me say a few words about my views on exchange-rate changes and the way they work out.

Bob's main emphasis, if I am not mistaken, was that the balance of trade would not improve. He mentioned money illusion as the major reason for this conclusion. But purely on a factual level, I think there is any amount of evidence from numerous devaluations in the past that the balance of trade frequently did improve. Purely on the factual level, I don't think that Bob can seriously claim that the balance of trade typically fails to improve after devaluation.

But this is not the whole story. I think it needs to be said very clearly that the effect of a devaluation cannot be adequately measured in this particular way. If one wants to find out what happens as a consequence of an exchange-rate change, one really has to do some work; one just can't simply look at what happened to the balance of trade. In any case, I'm not even clear that the balance of trade is a very useful indicator of the success of devaluation, unless one is thinking of devaluation as necessarily a measure that is aimed at improving the trade balance. If the problem is defined that way, of course, one wouldn't have any quarrel.

But one really shouldn't define the problem this way, because many countries postpone devaluation through all kinds of devices—quantitative restrictions, import taxes, export subsidies and the like—and when devaluation finally occurs, these devices are frequently scrapped or at least greatly reduced in scope. Since many devaluations take place essentially as tidying-up mechanisms which get rid of the substitute devices that have been used in the meantime, it should be clear, I think, that the balance of trade is not necessarily a good indicator of the success of a devaluation.

But there is another point regarding the balance of trade. Devaluation is often undertaken to increase export earnings, and the increase in export earnings may make possible a substantial increase in imports. In such cases, the trade balance may remain unchanged, but this clearly does not mean that the devaluation has been unsuccessful. Quite the contrary.

Chairman THORP: Walter Salant has asked for the last word on this subject.

SALANT: I would like to expand a little on what I said earlier. Bob Mundell argues that devaluations don't work any more because money illusion has vanished from the earth, with the result that wages in the devaluing country rise by as much as the price of foreign currencies. I have already commented that if only tradable goods rise in price by that percentage, the overall cost of living will rise by less, so that even a wage rise that fully offsets the rise in the cost of living will offset the devaluation only partially. That point takes into account a loss of money illusion only on the part of wage-earners, and I want to supplement it by considering two other points raised by Bob's argument: first, the implications for the effectiveness of devaluation of complete—not just partial—loss of money illusion; and, second, the truth of his statement that money illusion in this complete sense has disappeared.

As to the first point, a complete absence of what is called "money illusion" means that everything is determined in real terms. In that case, of course, Bob is correct; obviously, no monetary change can affect anything real. But that is tautology.

The interesting question then becomes the second one: whether it is true that the absence of money illusion is complete. That question really is not hard to answer if we recognize what it implies. One implication is that all money contracts have escalator clauses, which we know is far from true. But even if we leave that aside and assume that all income payments and debt obligations do have escalator clauses, the conclusion does not follow, because complete absence of money illusion implies still more. If all commodity and factor prices rose by the same proportion as the prices of foreign currencies—but the nominal stock of money rose by less—the real value of the money stock would be reduced. Therefore, the assumption that everything is determined in real terms implies that the monetary authorities increase the money supply by the same percentage that foreign currencies have risen in price. I don't think anybody would argue that the U. S. authorities propose to do that, unless they are kidding us about wanting to end the payments deficit. Assuming that they don't increase the money supply by that percentage, some degree of money illusion, or money effect, persists in the system; it is not really "illusion" but a sophisticated decision to change the predevaluation real variables.

If the money supply does not rise as much as the prices of foreign currencies, other prices and wages can rise in that proportion only if the discrepancy is entirely absorbed by a decline in the real value of the money stock. That result is very improbable. It is much more likely that the public will want to distribute its real loss between its holdings of money balances and other things, so that the discrepancy will be reflected only partly in a decline in the real value of the money supply.

From this I draw two conclusions. First, while it may be true that it now takes a bigger devaluation to get a given reduction in a deficit than it did before, it is not true that devaluation cannot reduce a deficit. Second, and more important, one cannot say anything about the effectiveness of a devaluation without specifying something about monetary policy.

V. KEY ISSUES IN THE DESIGN OF REFORM

*John Parke Young and
Members of the Conference*

The second day of the conference was devoted to a dialogue on what perhaps is best described as the "design of reform." The discussion reflected sharp differences of opinion both with regard to the architecture of the future international monetary system and with regard to the rules which should govern the system's operation. Much of the dialogue was concerned with the future role of the various means of international settlement—gold, the reserve currencies, SDRs, and possibly new forms—and with the question of how convertible these media should be into one another. Considerable attention was given to the issue of "symmetry" raised by Robert Solomon in his opening statement. As on the first day, the subject of exchange rates emerged on occasion, but from a different perspective. The first-day dialogue on exchange rates, reproduced in Chapter IV, was concerned with the effectiveness of rate changes; the references to exchange rates on the second day were concerned with questions of exchange-rate policy, particularly as related to the issue of symmetry. This chapter covers the morning session.

R. H.

Chairman THORP: I'm not sure that we all realized yesterday how favorable the immediate effect of our discussion would be, but, as you all know, the dollar has strengthened, and Mr. Volcker was reported this morning to have announced that the U. S. balance of payments will be corrected, not within one year, but certainly within two.

ROBERT TRIFFIN: Just in time for our next conference!

Chairman THORP: Our discussion on exchange rates yesterday was particularly interesting because it paid almost no attention to what one might call exchange-rate instruments or machinery. This may be in part because there is not very much left to talk about in this field after all the discussions of recent years. Our discussion dealt with matters that might more appropriately be called key issues than technical issues. Nevertheless, one of the subjects which comes up again and again is the question of how settlements should be made, and that brings us back to gold, dollars, SDRs, IOUs, Who-Owes-You's, and such matters. One of our more ambitious reformers in this area is John Parke Young, and I am asking him to start our discussion.

JOHN PARKE YOUNG: In looking at the problem of international monetary reform, I am impressed with the very many difficulties we face in developing an adequate international monetary system. In the past, progress has generally come only as a result of distress and crises. The question now is whether the situation is sufficiently bad—and is recognized as such—to make possible the difficult political decisions that are needed if we are to have an effective system.

Current planning gives insufficient attention, I believe, to the needs of private trade and investment. These needs are not going to be met unless reform goes farther than presently contemplated. Our recent crises are dramatic examples of trouble coming largely from the private sector; and, in the last analysis, it is the well-being of the private sector, both here and abroad, that is the object of monetary reform. Planning a stable currency that is available only to central banks is looking at only a part of the problem. The private sector also needs a reliable medium for its transactions—a stable international currency.

Much of the trouble today results from the fact that we do not have a satisfactory stable standard of value or medium of exchange for international transactions. Such a medium is being proposed for central banks in the form of a transferable reserve asset, but private traders and investors are not to have access to it. The IMF's excellent report on monetary reform dismisses in one sentence the subject of a medium for private transactions, referring to it as something for the "distant future." The future is already here, but some of us don't seem to know it. Our immediate problems make the strongest possible case for comprehensive reform.

Historically, gold, sterling, and the dollar were all available to the private sector for international transactions. Each in turn became unsatisfactory, and there is now a void in this important area. It is abundantly clear that no national currency can serve satisfactorily as an international currency either for central banks or for private trade.

The practical question, of course, is whether it is feasible to create a new form of international currency available to all. As I have just said, many feel that the world is not yet ready for such a currency and that we should begin by confining our efforts to a currency for central banks. I do not find this limitation convincing or, in fact, realistic. As I proposed in Bologna two years ago, it is time to take concrete measures for establishing an international currency available to all. The IMF could provide the world with such a currency by the simple device of opening an account for Fund members with transferable credits in terms of a new unit, perhaps equal to the SDR. These transferable credits would be obtained by central banks through the deposit of gold, eligible foreign exchange, SDRs, and other appropriate assets.

This plan is similar to proposals for a composite reserve asset or for a reserve-settlement account. But it goes a step further—a vital step—in that the credits would be available to commercial banks and, through them, to the public. Commercial banks could maintain accounts at their central banks in terms of the new unit. The commercial banks would acquire such credits at the central banks in exchange for local currency. The IMF credits thus would be available for international transactions. They would be transferrable by check as are ordinary bank deposits.

This credit currency would make its way into use gradually, as demanded. It would be designed to supplement and eventually to replace dollars and other national currencies for international transactions. Participation would be voluntary, at least initially, in order to expedite adoption of the proposal. The plan could be initiated by a few countries. Other countries would soon find it in their interest to participate. The currency could be defined in terms of gold, but it would not be redeemable in gold, although a country withdrawing from the arrangement could receive back the gold it had deposited.

This raises the question of the future of gold and the question of whether central banks would be willing to deposit gold if the deposit price were below the market price. If no gold were deposited, no serious harm would be done. Gold is already on the shelf as a means of international settlement because of price uncertainties.

The SDR could continue until the new currency became well established, but it should eventually be abolished, with reserve creation thereafter made in the form of transferable credits.

An international currency available to the private sector would help solve a number of problems. Take, for example, the adjustment problem. As the use of such a currency expanded, the adjustment of exchange rates would be a less disturbing matter. The reason is that rate changes would affect fewer transactions. This would encourage more frequent rate changes, thus avoiding serious departures from international equilibrium. An exchange adjustment would become more of a national matter, although it would still, of course, have international aspects.

An international currency would reduce the adjustment problem to more of a national matter. Proposals for sanctions against surplus countries would become less important. Since an international currency would facilitate exchange-rate adjustments, it would be easier for a country to pursue a full-employment policy without external repercussions.

Finally, an international currency would help relieve the problem of short-term capital movements. The main reason why corporations, banks, and others shift funds from one currency into another, apart from interest-rate differentials, is uncertainty regarding the future pattern of exchange rates. Such shifts in funds are not always successful, and financial statements commonly include an item, "loss from currency depreciation." Since an international currency would be more stable than national currencies subject to balance-of-payments difficulties, it would reduce the incentive to shift funds. It would tend to replace the uncontrolled and "stateless" Eurodollar, which is now under no national or international control.

As we look ahead to a European currency, and thus to two large currency blocs, the adjustment of exchange rates between the blocs becomes a matter of major consequence. A needed adjustment between the dollar and the European currency would be a political question of who adjusts to whom—a problem which could easily lead to postponement of necessary action. An international currency would facilitate such an adjustment.

There would be various other advantages. An international currency would promote a worldwide liberal trading community by making unnecessary many defensive protectionist devices. The developing countries would be aided by a currency which did not tie them to a particular bloc but facilitated access to the world market. An international currency would also contribute to beneficial economic relations between the communist and noncommunist countries. Such a currency would be helpful in view of the Soviet use of gold and the difficulties regarding settlement in gold.

A new and unfamiliar credit instrument of course requires time for confidence and general acceptability to develop. It must contend with traditional means of payment and payment practices. But an IMF currency would have important pluses in its favor. With over twenty-five years of successful operation behind it, the International Monetary Fund enjoys widespread respect. It has strong assets, and its credit standing is high. An IMF currency, moreover, would have behind it dollars and other leading currencies carrying exchange-rate guarantees. Convertibility could be offered in a package of such currencies or in any from a list of available currencies.

I believe that an international currency issued by the IMF would be well received. Usage could expand quickly. Growth of the Eurodollar market took place rapidly, and has abundantly illustrated the need for an international currency.

We face, however, the usual resistance to innovation. The SDR, as we all know, had to overcome strong opposition. Changes in the international monetary system must be acceptable to central bankers, who are inclined to be highly cautious. Adequate reform is not going to come easily; the Federal Reserve System and the International Monetary Fund both met strong resistance from the banking community. But something along the lines I've indicated is greatly needed, and I am persuaded that it will come sooner or later. There is no satisfactory alternative.

Chairman THORP: Thank you, John. After a day when the word "pessimism" has been used so often, it is rather nice to have this display of optimism.

YOUNG: I'm not too optimistic, Willard—at least in the short run.

Chairman THORP: Well, it requires a lot of optimism even to make your proposal.

One of the subjects about which we all talk at great length, in spite of the fact that we have little knowledge about it, is the SDR. We must see just where it fits into the picture. To introduce this complicated subject, I think it would be helpful if we asked Frank Southard to tell us whatever he can about how the new creation actually is behaving.

FRANK A. SOUTHARD, JR.: I will try to be brief and factual. First, let me say a few words about how SDRs work. As you all know, the SDR has now been in operation for more than three years, and as a practical matter—John Exter to the contrary notwithstanding—it has worked very smoothly. The so-called "designation process" has been smooth. Every quarter, the Fund staff brings before the Board a designation schedule in which the stronger countries are listed and in which anticipated transactions in SDRs during the quarter are allocated schematically among these countries. Once the schedule has been approved by the Board and it has been determined that no country is objecting to being designated, the treasurer of the Fund, when some country wants to use SDRs, can quickly make the appropriate calculations and send the cables out right away.

This has been a very fast process. There have been no delays. There is no right of challenge. Countries have to certify that they have a need to use SDRs. They cannot use SDRs simply for the purpose of changing the composition of their reserves, but the Fund has no right to challenge their declarations. There is a post facto audit—a careful audit—to determine whether, in fact, the country did have a need to use SDRs, and there have been a very few cases where a country used SDRs even though it was determined later that the country did not need to use them. One or two cases of that sort involved countries which, after making the decision to use SDRs, experienced a sudden improvement in their payments positions; they knew themselves that they really shouldn't have used SDRs.

Well, we don't embarrass them. A reverse transaction is very quietly carried out. But such cases are very rare. Countries have been quite willing to hold SDRs; indeed, instead of there being any reluctance to hold them, there has been a general eagerness to acquire more SDRs through the designation process. There has been no evidence whatever of any country rushing to use SDRs in preference to other reserve assets that it might have.

So all of this has worked out about as one would hope, and from the beginning there has been a reasonably good understanding of how this man-made international asset could be used. As expected, there have been a number of cases where one country, with the consent of a second country, has used SDRs to make a payment to that second country outside of the designation scheme.

The attractiveness of the SDR as a reserve asset is enhanced by the fact that it can be used to settle a country's obligations to the Fund. Countries can pay interest or service charges, and can even repay Fund drawings with SDRs. The Fund has acquired substantial amounts of SDRs in this way, and has used SDRs in some cases to make payments to Fund members.

Let me now say a few words about the "reconstitution" process. We economists have a bent for hatching up difficult words to describe simple things; reconstitution is really just another word for repayment of SDRs. The problem of repayment arose because, in the long and tortuous negotiations leading to the creation of the SDR, there were two factions. There was a faction that wanted the SDR to be regarded as a reserve asset and—this may please John Exter—to have reserve qualities such as to make it as nearly gold-like as possible. The other faction, led by the French, wanted the SDR to be a credit instrument. This faction would really have liked to have had 100 percent repayment after a period of time, just as Fund drawings are subject to complete repayment after a period of time. Well, as usually happens in such negotiations, a compromise was worked out. The compromise was that a country is supposed to maintain on the basis of rather complicated calculations a balance in its SDR account of not less than 30 percent of its cumulative allocation of SDRs.

During the first couple of years, there were no reconstitution problems. But we are now reaching a point where some reconstitution is called for, and although certain countries, particularly the less developed countries, don't like reconstitution—and neither do I nor, indeed, hardly anybody anymore—the requirement is still in force, and countries are taking it in their stride.

This brings me to the subject of future SDR allocations. The Fund Articles provide that annual allocations will take place during a basic period, these allocations being subject to change up or down during the basic period. The first basic period was three years, although the norm is supposed to be five, and the total allocations, as you may recall, amounted to $9.4 billion, with $3.4 billion the first year and about $3 billion apiece the next two. There has been no allocation for the new basic period which began on January 1, 1973. The reason for that, I think, is the reason Mr. Schleiminger suggested: that there is a controversy over whether there is too much liquidity in the world—whether there is a need for any more SDRs at this time. The factions in this controversy have thus far held their lines fairly tightly, and the Fund's Managing Director, who is required under the Fund Articles to determine whether he thinks there should be a new allocation and also to determine through consultation whether there is a consensus in favor of it, has not been able to determine such a consensus. As a result, there has been no new allocation.

I have no way of knowing when this picture will change. There have been fewer cries of outrage than I would have thought. Although the standstill has undoubtedly been disappointing to a number of countries, the situation seems on the whole—again— to have been taken in stride. Of course, the Managing Director can make a proposal at any time. He could make it next week or he could make it two years from now, but in the meantime we are living in what we call a "zero basic period." The fact that we are in a zero period doesn't mean, of course, that the SDR system has come to a halt; countries still have SDRs and can use them. I don't think I want to express any personal opinion of what is right and what is wrong in this dispute. As is usual in such debates, there is something to be said on both sides.

I might now say just a word about possible reforms in the SDR system. Bob Solomon spoke of this, and I will quickly list some of the matters that I think will have to be considered if the SDR is to be properly equipped for future evolution.

First, there is the "reconstitution" question. I think there is every evidence of a very wide consensus in favor of eliminating completely the obligation to reconstitute.

Second, there is the question of what interest rate should be paid on excess balances in the SDR account and by countries that have used SDRs. The account of course always balances out, but the Fund earns interest on its own acquisitions of SDRs. The rate of interest at present is very low, and I think it is likely that there will be a consensus that if the SDR is to compete properly with other reserve assets, it will need to have a better return. Perhaps the best way of dealing with this matter is to see that the Fund has adequate authority to change the rate from time to time.

The third area of possible reform concerns the method of SDR allocation. The present method of allocation is in proportion to Fund quotas. Under this system, Paraguay, for example, gets an amount of SDRs, out of any total allocated, equal to its percentage share of total Fund quotas. This system is regarded by the less developed countries as a rather unfair basis for allocation. Indeed, such countries don't like the formula which governs the determination of Fund quotas themselves; they feel that the formula gives the developed countries too much of a shake. In any case, the method of SDR allocation will clearly need to be examined in any comprehensive discussion of reform.

Let me now turn to the possibility of extending the use of SDRs to types of users beyond those currently authorized to engage in SDR transactions. At the present time, the Fund Articles limit transactions in SDRs to the monetary authorities—central banks or treasuries—of member countries and to one or two other institutions, such as the Bank for International Settlements. There are precious few institutions in the world outside of central banks and member-country treasuries that can be holders of SDRs. The simplest thing in my view that can be done is to make the "other holder" definition very broad indeed. I see almost no reason why it should not be possible for anybody or any institution to be a holder of SDRs if the Fund so decides.

Now this, of course, could open the way for a nonorganic type of "link" proposal, for if the International Development Association or the Inter-American Bank or the Asian Bank could hold SDRs, which they cannot today, then it would be open to the developed countries to instruct the Fund to hand over some of their new allocations of SDRs to such institutions. This, in my view, could be a way in which the world might feel its way toward a link.

In this connection, I might say that it would be wrong to assume that there is a monolithic position within the less developed world on this question of the link. There is a considerable number of what I would call successful developing countries—countries like Mexico, Malaysia, or Venezuela, that have been pretty successful in maintaining stable price levels and in building up their reserves—which have a strong suspicion that if there is a link, they are not going to receive any of these SDRs because they will be considered too well off for such assistance. Such countries would like to have a better distribution of SDRs, but not necessarily via a link proposal.

Finally, let me comment on the possibility raised by John Parke Young regarding a much wider use of SDRs than is presently authorized. I think the only quick answer I would want to give is that of course this can be done. How fast the evolution can take place is very difficult to forecast. Perhaps the simplest first step one could imagine would be to allow big banks, such as the big banks in New York or the Bank of America, to acquire SDRs from the Federal Reserve Banks themselves. In this way, SDRs could be developed into a more important means of international settlement. To push the idea further, I do not find it difficult conceptually to contemplate a broad use of SDRs as a means of payment, but I do think that this is way down the road. It does seem to me that SDRs at some point could be developed to the point where they could be an intervention currency and that in the evolution we might actually reach the point where the dollar would have all of the rights and privileges of other currencies, including the possibility of floating. Until something like that happens, I fail to see how the U. S. dollar can float.

Sir ROY HARROD: Why can't the dollar float? The dollar is simply a currency and, if other currencies can float, the dollar surely can. I would be interested in Mr. Southard's reactions.

SOUTHARD: As long as the dollar remains the intervention currency, I do not see how it can independently float.

Chairman THORP: A number of members have asked for the floor. The first is John Exter.

JOHN EXTER: This is the fourth Bologna-Claremont conference and also my fourth. I happen to be a believer in the gold standard—in short, a "gold bug." There was a sprinkling of others at the first Bologna conference. Jacques Rueff was at the first and second Bologna conferences, the late Michael Heilperin was at the first Claremont conference, but here I find myself alone, unless there is a golden nugget around this table that I have not yet turned up. So you can imagine how my heart leaped yesterday morning when our distinguished Moderator, for the first time at these conferences, took a close look at the barbaric but brightly shining— even glittering—gold-standard bridge across our Slough of Despond. He walked toward it, thought the fields on the other side looked a little greener, even took a gingerly step or two on it to see whether it would bear his weight, looked over his shoulder to see whether his friends were watching—and then stepped back to try at a later time.

Needless to say, I crossed the bridge long ago. At each of these conferences, I have sounded the alarm. I have tried to identify the problem, and I think I can say with some justification that events have vindicated me. After the first Bologna conference, central banks closed the gold window to private people. After the first Claremont conference, we had what I would call a severe liquidity squeeze in dollars. Treasury bills went up to 8 percent, the prime rate to 8.5 percent, the Eurodollar rate to 12 percent, the Dow Jones average to 631, and Penn Central to the bankruptcy court. After the second Bologna conference, President Nixon closed the gold window to central banks.

Much as I enjoy these conferences, I do have my frustrations. My model is different from those of other economists. Having rejected Keynes, having never accepted Friedman, and having left the academic world, I find I have a communications problem. I think more in terms of debtor-creditor relationships, which never get on the agenda, and of interest rates, which are seldom mentioned.

So four years ago in this room, I built an upside-down pyramid. It is in Randall's book, The Economics of International Adjustment (this will be my only commercial). In essence, it was an inverted pyramid of credit erected on a block of gold at the base. I pointed out two principal constraints: first, that currencies in it were locked together at fixed exchange rates and were convertible, at least by central banks, into U. S. gold at $35 an ounce; and, second, that each debtor in it was required to pay his debts. I foresaw the breakdown of both of these constraints. I thought my message was clear at the time, but I was wrong. Bob Mundell said he understood my pyramid, and then proceeded to say that the base should be dollars, not gold, and that I had overemphasized gold—which indicated that he had not understood me at all.

I shall therefore make my point again in even plainer English, if I can. The pyramid shows that there is a fundamental difference between good commodity store-of-value money—like gold—and paper IOU money. John Law was only the first in modern times to argue that the authorities, by issuing paper instead of relying on specie, could somehow cheat nature and get something for nothing. John Law got his big Mississippi Bubble; we have our gigantic upside-down pyramid. I was worried about its size even four years ago, and I was even more worried about its explosive growth, for the pyramid shape is just another way of saying that debt in the world is growing at an exponential rate.

Four years ago, I did not know which of the two constraints would go first. Actually, it proved to be the convertibility constraint; the tie to gold disappeared on August 15, 1971. With it went the chief obstacle to the growth of the pyramid. So today this growth is more explosive than ever. At this conference, I am concerned about the second constraint: Whether debtors in general can continue to pay their debts—especially the least liquid at the top of the pyramid, who have borrowed short and lent or invested long.

August 15, 1971 was a watershed date. Before then, a dollar bill said, in effect, "I owe you gold at $35 an ounce," if the "you" was a central bank. Since that date, a dollar bill says, "I owe you nothing." And this is true, not just of the dollar, but of all currencies. No central bank pays any other today in good store-of-value money. All, in effect, are bankrupt.

So today, "IOU-nothings" are trading, minute by minute, against all the others in the foreign-exchange markets of the world. No wonder people are confused and uncertain about which IOU-nothings to buy on any given day. In an IOU-nothing world, in which no central bank pays, the advantage to each lies in lowering the value of its IOU-nothings in relation to those of the rest. This situation cheapens its goods abroad, stimulates exports, discourages imports, and helps economic activity. It also helps the home folks to have more IOU-nothings in their paychecks. Maybe that's the real money illusion.

So since August 15, 1971, the name of the game has fundamentally changed. An important incentive to maintain an exchange rate is gone. We are now in a world of competitive exchange-rate depreciation, which means competitive monetary expansion, which in turn means worldwide inflation on a scale hitherto unknown in history. It also means a world of floating exchange rates, with IOU-nothings growing rapidly in all countries, but more rapidly in some than in others.

It is idle for any central bank to think that it can keep the value of its own IOU-nothings constant, or even nearly constant, in relation to all the others for very long. So if Bob Solomon thinks, as I understood him to say yesterday, that international monetary reform can take us back to some reasonably stable exchange-rate system, he might as well banish the thought and pack up. In particular, I would advise him to banish the thought of the SDR. It has no obligor, so it is not even an IOU-nothing; it is a "who owes you nothing?" And the thought of an IOU-nothing pyramid on a who-owes-you-nothing base is not one that I can keep in my head for very long.

You can see why I thought the exchange-rate discussion yesterday was irrelevant and sterile. No country today can have an exchange-rate policy. If anyone tries to cop out of the competitive exchange-rate depreciation race, as the Swiss are trying to do now, the value of their IOU-nothings will rise in the marketplace. For in a world of rapidly depreciating IOU-nothings, appreciating IOU-nothings draw buyers as honey draws flies. An appreciating exchange rate is intolerable domestically, so the central bank will be forced to resume expansionism.

So where do we go from here? The problem today is not exchange rates or central bank reserves; it is the debt in the pyramid. There is a great deal that can never be repaid—particularly that debt owed by the illiquid debtors at the top—and it is in all currencies. It is currently being paid only because all central banks are seeing to it that new debt in their currencies is being created fast enough to enable the old debt to be serviced and repaid. No central bank dares to stop its expansionism for fear of the consequences. They are all locked in—prisoners of their own expansionism.

But we all know that the pyramid cannot go on growing forever. Interest rates rise, and become the killers. There must somehow, someday, be a liquidation. I see it occurring in either of two ways. One is through market forces taking over from the authorities. Thus far we have only a Penn Central disaster here and a Rolls Royce disaster there, but if one of these ever starts to snowball, and if the snowball begins to hit our financial institutions that have borrowed short and lent long, the authorities could find it impossible to stop the situation. Economic activity would collapse, and the central bank would soon find itself pushing on a string instead of loosening the reins. This is the 1929-33 kind of liquidation.

The other kind is that in which the authorities somehow manage to keep the pyramid growing. But then the central bank IOU-nothings at last really become worth nothing—they are not worth a continental. So all debts in them, in effect, are then extinguished, and the authorities must think up a new currency and start all over again. After all this happens, I hope that our Moderator will by then have crossed the gold-standard bridge and, in his persuasive way, will have convinced the major governments of the world to do so too. On that optimistic note—for I really am, as you all know, a great optimist—I thank you.

ROBERT W. OLIVER: It is difficult to follow John Exter's picturesque presentation exposing IOU-nothings, though I hope that we can build an international system on "IOU-somethings" other than gold.

Let me begin with a few words about exchange-rate policy. Under the Bretton Woods system, changes in the relative values of the major currencies have usually taken place in an atmosphere of crisis, for in a crisis a government can claim that it has no choice. But this only reveals a major deficiency in the Bretton Woods system: since "fundamental disequilibrium" was never clearly defined, exchange-rate adjustment has never been automatic. Indeed, rate adjustment has frequently been delayed until a really substantial change was necessary—a problem which has been mitigated, but not solved, by the wider bands used since the Smithsonian agreement.

There are, I think, three possible solutions. First, we could return to a rigidly fixed exchange-rate system, it being accepted that balance-of-payments problems will always be solved, at least for the major powers, by internal income and price adjustments. Second, we could adopt a system of floating exchange rates. Third, we could move toward a semi-fixed-rate system which has a built-in, more or less automatic, and therefore nonpolitical exchange-rate adjustment mechanism.

I doubt that the first of these alternatives is practical for the whole world, since the world is not an optimum currency area, even though it might eventually be possible for regions larger than nations—for example, the European Economic Community or the United States plus Canada—to accept a single monetary authority. As was pointed out yesterday, however, regional comparative advantage may change, regional growth rates may differ substantially, and cyclical income changes may not synchronize. In these cases, the required shifts in relative regional price levels may be easier to arrange through exchange-rate changes than through internal price or income changes.

I suspect that floating currencies, the second alternative, will become less the exception and more the rule in the foreseeable future, particularly if an automatic adjustment mechanism cannot be added to a modified Bretton Woods system. But the danger, so eloquently described by Lord Robbins, of greater inflation and of trade and capital controls would, I think, be increased, which means that floating rates will not be a satisfactory permanent solution.

The preferable alternative, it seems to me, is a sliding key-currency parity system, coupled, perhaps, with a new international medium of exchange along the lines suggested by John Parke Young. The crucial issue in any event is agreement on an automatic exchange-rate adjustment mechanism for major currencies, free from undue political pressure. The current American proposal for the automatic appreciation or depreciation of key currencies, depending on the acquisition of too great, or the reduction to too small, a stock of international reserves, seems to me a promising solution—provided, of course, that supplementary fiscal and monetary policies are included in each package, and provided also that full employment without undue inflation is accepted as the correct macroeconomic policy for each major regional bloc. This is essentially the "prong proposal" which I first heard from Professor Triffin in this very room four years ago.

Assuming that such a policy would make sense, there is still the problem of deciding for each region what level of reserves is correct. This problem is not unlike determining the proper quotas for members of the International Monetary Fund, though in some ways it is more complicated. It is particularly complicated if we suppose that the reserves of the low-income countries should be supplemented more or less continuously by some sort of permanent aid from the high-income countries of the world.

When the subject of aid and the creation of SDRs was mentioned by Lord Robbins yesterday, he concluded that the two matters should not be mixed. I believe I understand the argument, but I think the subject needs further discussion, for the second "decade of development" may well be stillborn if grant-type assistance depends entirely on the goodwill of governments elected by people who are tired of the international struggle and anxious to retreat behind national boundaries. Beyond this, there is the question of the rate at which international reserve assets should increase, and there is, of course, the question of which national currencies, if any, should supplement gold and SDRs in any formula used to trigger automatic exchange-rate changes. These issues, I think, are worth considerable additional discussion.

Chairman THORP: It would be quite an incomplete international monetary conference if we did not all carry away a statistical table provided by Robert Triffin. We now have one before us, and I think we should ask Bob to explain its significance.

TRIFFIN: I don't think my table adds very much to what we know, but perhaps it puts our knowledge in a broader perspective. The table was inspired by my conviction that, while I welcome the emphasis put on the process of adjustment rather than on the process of reserve creation, I think the two are intimately linked. I certainly welcome the U.S. proposal for a "fork" or "prong" on reserve levels and, as Professor Oliver was kind enough to remember, this is exactly the proposal I made here four years ago. I am a little worried, however, about some of the accompanying comments—particularly the comment that the use of reserve currencies should be "neither generally banned nor encouraged." While this formula is unexceptionable, I still think that something has to be done about reserve currencies. They were neither banned nor encouraged over the last twenty-five years, yet we find ourselves in the situation which is briefly described in my table.

As far as the mechanism of adjustment is concerned, there is no doubt in my mind that the major culprits have been the reserve-currency countries. Other countries in deficit cannot continue in deficit very long; they are forced to adjust. It is true that the surplus countries can delay indefinitely an upward revaluation of their currencies or other adjustment measures, but it would be very difficult to argue that the major source of international disequilibrium has been the excessively deflationary policies of the surplus countries. They may not have been willing to catch up with the general inflation of other countries, but the basic problem lies else-

SOURCES AND DISTRIBUTION OF WORLD MONETARY RESERVES, 1949-72

(in billions of dollars)

	End of			Changes	
	1949	1969	Sept. 1972	1950-9/72	1970-9/72
I. World Monetary Gold = Net Reserves of:	35.0	41.0	44.9[1]	+9.9[1]	+3.9[1]
A. United States	22.7	-0.1	-49.3	-72.0	-49.2
1. Assets	26.0	17.0	13.2	-12.8	-3.8
2. Liabilities	-3.4	-17.0	-62.5	-59.3	-45.5
B. Other Countries	12.4	47.9	121.2	+108.8	+73.3
1. Assets	19.5	61.2	137.7	+118.2	+76.5
2. Liabilities	-7.1	-13.4	-16.6	-9.5	-3.2
C. Undetermined[2]	-0.1	-6.8	-26.9	-26.8	-20.1
II. Credit Reserves = -(IA2+IB2+IC)	10.5	37.2	106.0	+95.5	+68.8
A. Reserve Currencies	10.4	32.4	96.0	+85.6	+63.6
B. SDRs	-	-	10.1[3]	+10.1[3]	+10.1[3]
C. IMF, EF, BIS credits	0.1	4.8	-	-0.1	-4.8
III. Gross Reserves = I+II=IA1+IB1	45.5	78.2	151.0	+105.5	+72.8

FOOTNOTES:
1. Of which $3.5 billion is from dollar devaluation of December 1971.
2. Undistributed IMF profits, minus unallocated reserve liabilities, roughly half of which (44% at end of 1971) are estimated to be U.S. liabilities.
3. Of which $0.8 billion is from dollar devaluation of December 1971.

SOURCE: IMF International Financial Statistics, tables on international reserves.

Prepared by Robert Triffin

where. What emerges most strikingly is that the U. S. payments deficit since 1949 comes to a total of something like $80 billion. This almost incredible result could not have happened if the great bulk of the deficit—recently 90 percent or more—had not been financed simply by the use of the dollar as a reserve currency.

I cannot for the life of me see how we can pretend to deal with the problem of adjustment without facing this startling fact. In the last three years alone, gross international reserves have just about doubled. What does that doubling mean? It means that as much reserves were added to the world reserve pool in three years as were created prior to that time in all the years since Adam and Eve. I think this should be one of the key issues in any international monetary discussion; as long as we don't face that fact, we are writing Hamlet without any role for the Prince of Denmark.

Chairman THORP: Your reference to Adam and Eve reminds me that, for a period, Adam and Eve had no reserves at all. Bob Solomon has asked for a minute.

ROBERT SOLOMON: I do not really disagree with Robert's major conclusion, but I would offer a slightly different perspective. If we look at the period from the end of 1949 to the end of 1969, we find that reserve-currency expansion averaged only about $1 billion a year, which is rather moderate; it is only 2 percent or so of world reserves at the beginning of the period. The big expansion came in the past three years—1970, 1971, and 1972. This was the period when the adjustment process really broke down. It was the failure of the adjustment process that led to the enormous speculative outflow of funds from the United States; if the adjustment process had worked properly, we would not have had this enormous increase in reserve creation.

HARROD: Just one word. In those three years, the main increase of dollars in world reserves were dollars that had previously been held by private parties. These private parties—individuals, companies, banks, and so on—turned their dollars into the central bank. They said, "We don't want to hold these dollars any more." That was the main cause of the reserve increase.

WALTER S. SALANT: Like Bob Solomon, I don't disagree with the main thrust of Robert Triffin's remarks, but I want to make a comment that's only about 98 percent facetious: it is also true that the number of economists created in recent years exceeds the entire number previously created since Adam and Eve!

FRITZ MACHLUP: I want to find out about Triffin's second footnote, which refers to U. S. liabilities. I am not clear whether he means dollar liabilities or U. S. liabilities, which need not be the same.

TRIFFIN: I took that figure from the last annual report of the Fund, which refers to the liabilities as U. S. liabilities, including Eurodollar liabilities.

MACHLUP: Eurodollars are not U. S. liabilities.

TRIFFIN: They are claims on the United States by foreign central banks held via . . .

MACHLUP: They are not claims against the United States; they are claims against European banks.

TRIFFIN: Well, let's take a simple case. Italy has, let us say, deposits at the Chase in New York, then shifts the deposits to a branch of Chase in London. At that point, the deposits disappear as a liability of the United States according to your way of understanding the situation. To my mind, the ultimate debtor as well as the ultimate creditor are the same in both cases, and I think it is an exaggeration to say that the deposits are no longer a U. S. liability.

Chairman THORP: This definitional disagreement is now clear, and I will turn to John Exter.

EXTER: I would like to zero in a little bit on the adjustment process.

Chairman THORP: You can't do that in one minute, can you?

EXTER: Yes I can. At Bologna, Fritz Machlup made a suggestion which captivated me—that the German central bank should put its dollars on deposit at the Federal Reserve and sterilize them there. I pointed out to him that he was coming very close to the adjustment process under the gold standard and that if he took just one more step—namely, to permit the German central bank to use those deposits to buy U. S. gold— he would have an effective adjustment process, and I would welcome him to the gold standard club. I think that is the key; a gold loss must contract the reserves of the losing central bank, and a gold gain must expand the reserves of the gaining central bank.

ROBERT A. MUNDELL: I have a point regarding the exchange between Robert Triffin and Fritz Machlup. At the last Bologna conference, we discussed in detail matters relating to dollar liabilities and Eurodollars. It seems to me that we need to divide these liabilities into three categories: first, liabilities of banks in the United States; second, Eurodollar liabilities of overseas branches of American banks; and third, Eurodollar liabilities of banks that are European in origin. It is very important to distinguish between the second and third categories, because the American overseas bank has access to the Federal Reserve as a lender of last resort, whereas banks of European origin do not.

Let me conclude with a remark about world money. John Exter says it's gold, Frank Southard says it will be SDRs, and I say it's still dollars—although some other currencies are coming to the forefront and a European currency is a new possibility. What we should all be trying to solve at this meeting is what should be the numeraire of the world system if it is not to continue to be the U. S. dollar. This seems to me the most fundamental problem of international monetary reform.

HENRY C. WALLICH: I agree with Bob Mundell that dollar liabilities should be split up into three parts, but the most significant division of Eurodollar liabilities, it seems to me, is between those Eurodollars backed by dollar assets in the United States and those backed by assets which are not liabilities of the United States.

Chairman THORP: We will expect next time a much more refined and sophisticated table from Robert Triffin. I don't envy him in that assignment. The next speaker is Peter Kenen.

PETER B. KENEN: First, let me say a word about this question of Eurodollars versus U. S. liabilities. Wherever one draws a line, the distinction and its implications are of enormous significance for any proposal to consolidate the so-called dollar overhang. Do we mean by consolidation the funding only of the obligations of U. S. banks and of the U. S. money market, or do we mean rather the elimination from the system of all currency holdings? If we mean the latter, what do we do to prevent a major collapse or disintegration of the entire Eurocurrency system? I have not thought my way through the problem, but it does seem to me important for any consolidation proposal, and I am worried about our failure thus far to discuss this point.

I agree with Bob Solomon that the enormous increase in dollar liabilities since 1969 reflects a breakdown of the adjustment mechanism. Even a well-functioning adjustment mechanism, however, may have to cope in the future with very large flows of volatile capital. We cannot leap to the millenium—the day on which the so-called speculators are absolutely convinced that the authorities are prepared to maintain whatever system they have chosen to adopt. And I am far from sure that any system one might devise involving asset settlements will have sufficient elasticity to deal with these flows. Whatever the reserve system we propose, we must provide for reserve supplements—reserve elasticity—that would allow the system to accommodate massive capital flows on a short-term basis. Otherwise, we must face quite frankly and bluntly the question of controlling capital movements. Either we must have sufficient elasticity in the system to accommodate massive capital flows or we must be prepared to restrict those capital flows. I'm not sure which way we ought to go. There seem to me serious problems on both sides.

Coming back to the broader issue—the choice of a reserve medium or reserve standard—it seems to me useful to distinguish among three basic views which do not correspond precisely to the conventional distinction between store of value, medium of exchange, and standard of value, but which do relate indirectly to those functions. Bob Mundell is right to remind us that we are talking about the basic functions of money.

There are some—and I think John Exter is among them— who look upon the ultimate international reserve asset as a safeguard against excessive national credit creation. John sees gold as having the necessary properties, because the supply of gold is more or less inelastic and more or less immune to manipulation by governments. The objection to such a standard, it seems to me, is not so much the implicit value judgment involved—that price stability comes first, that the sanctity of debtor obligations comes high in the order of priorities. It is rather a prudential objection. When there is a fundamental conflict between the rules of the game and the pursuit of national economic objectives, governments will not abide by the rules of the game; they will overthrow the standard. To predicate the monetary standard upon the naive supposition that governments will voluntarily subordinate their vital national objectives to any such abstract rule is to guarantee the failure of the standard, as it has been doomed to failure—if I too may cite history grandly—since Adam and Eve. I am simply repeating a point I made yesterday. We are obliged in our planning to think of a system that is robust against the misbehavior of governments, that does not rest on the assumption that governments will always behave in optimum fashion.

There is another view, extremely different from the view I have just outlined, which looks upon international reserves primarily as that mass of cash which governments have at their disposal to stabilize exchange rates—assets that deficit countries can sell to prevent their currencies from depreciating in the market. After all, surplus countries don't need reserves; they need only the power to print their own money to soak up the currency of the deficit country. On this view, the creation of reserves is a matter of accommodating the convenience of governments, providing them with the assets necessary to delay adjustment for whatever is deemed to be the appropriate length of time. I would suggest that the debate in the Committee of Twenty, summarized for us yesterday by Bob Solomon, focuses midway between these two views, and part of our task today is to ask whether it focuses too narrowly. Does it neglect the considerations which Bob Mundell and John Exter have raised by seeking in a different way to limit the freedom of governments? By limiting the freedom of governments to intervene in the exchange market, is the new consensus too much biased in favor of rapid adjustment and frequent exchange-rate changes rather than slow adjustment and the stability of exchange rates?

The intermediate set of considerations raised in the debates of the Committee of Twenty concentrates upon two functions of reserves. One function of reserves, or of movements in reserves, is to trigger adjustment. The mechanism may be automatic, as under the gold standard—where, as we are reminded by John Exter, outflows of reserves force monetary contraction and internal adjustment. Alternatively, reserve changes may be employed as indicators to compel consultation or action at the initiative of governments. The second function of the reserve system is to distribute obligations among governments—to determine whether we have a world of symmetrical settlement and symmetrical responses to imbalances or a system such as we have today involving the creation of reserve assets by one country. The rules governing the creation and use of reserves govern the degree to which the obligation to adjust is distributed among countries. In this connection, however, let us draw sharply the distinction between the burden of adjustment and the burden of initiating adjustment—a distinction that has been made often and forgotten even more often. My point here is that the primary burden is political. Who is forced to move, to admit by implication that he has made a mistake—these are the pragmatic and political aspects of reserve creation and transfer that have come to the fore in the Committee of Twenty. The debate appears to be focusing on the relationship between the reserve system and the adjustment mechanism—an emphasis which I deem to be long overdue.

Let me summarize by stating my concerns as questions. Which asset, or set of assets, best accomplishes whatever functions we want reserves to perform? What role do we assign to the SDR? And how do we get from where we are to where we want to be? How do we avoid mixing up the new rules of the game with the set of transitional rules which will be required to redistribute reserves so that the new system can run properly? These are the questions on my mind, and I hope we can address some of our discussion to them.

TIBOR SCITOVSKY: I was glad that we had the opportunity this morning to hear Mr. Southard's admirable survey of the SDR system, because it brings us back to a matter that was mentioned yesterday and then was more or less forgotten— namely, the desire for more symmetry in the international monetary system. I would like to make a few comments on that subject.

One of the reasons for this desire, of course, is the feeling on the part of some countries that the United States has had an unfair advantage under the dollar system. There is also a feeling in this country that the United States has had an unfair handicap under the same system. Another reason is that a more symmetrical arrangement would make it possible to change the dollar exchange rate in an atmosphere that might be less of a crisis nature. It is not easy to change the dollar rate except under conditions of crisis, which is one reason for the desire for a numeraire other than the dollar—although having a numeraire other than the dollar will not in itself provide us with a symmetrical system.

Another aspect of symmetry which I think is important relates to the role of central banks in maintaining currencies within the admissable range around parity. Here we have the well-known proposition that if we have N currencies and N central banks, we need N + 1 currencies if central banks are to avoid intervention conflicts in a symmetrical system. This is one reason why, in addition to the N national currencies, we may need an asset such as gold, SDRs, or whatever you like. There are ways of avoiding the need for an extra currency, but in a world of many countries the system would have to be very complicated if symmetry were to be achieved.

Under present arrangements, the dollar is the intervention currency, and we cannot have a symmetrical system, of course, as long as that situation continues. Here we might take a lesson from the Common Market countries, which have evolved symmetrical intervention techniques among themselves that appear to be working reasonably well. We might also explore the possible use of the SDR as an intervention currency, as Mr. Southard has suggested. Well, Mr. Chairman, I have raised questions which I don't feel competent to answer, but I do feel that they are important questions.

Chairman THORP: Randall Hinshaw would like to get into this discussion.

RANDALL HINSHAW: This is just a brief comment on Professor Scitovsky's remarks about symmetry in the foreign-exchange market. Robert Triffin, Guenther Schleiminger, and I were at one time or another Deputies on the Managing Board of the European Payments Union, and during the latter part of that period, the EPU established a symmetrical system of central bank intervention in the foreign-exchange market known as the intra-European arbitrage arrangement. Under this system, each participating central bank supported all the other participating currencies with its own currency at the agreed support points. That system worked very well, but the number of participants was small—only eight to begin with. With a large number of countries, a symmetrical arrangement of this kind might be impracticable. If we want a symmetrical system, another possibility, suggested both by Frank Southard and Tibor Scitovsky, would be to use the SDR as an intervention currency.

GUENTHER SCHLEIMINGER: Mr. Chairman, I would like to pursue Randall Hinshaw's reference to the historical experience of the European Payments Union. The EPU was an asset-settlement system; more accurately, it was a partial system of asset settlements. Balances accumulating monthly were settled partly in gold or dollars—dollars at that time were as good as gold—and partly in credit, and these balances were expressed in an abstract unit of account which was really the forerunner of the SDR.

I think that a transitional system somewhat along these lines would be possible these days, with only partial settlement. The system could start on a fifty-fifty basis and gradually harden until 100 percent convertibility were achieved. Now the EPU system worked, as Randall said, among a small number of countries, but if we count the countries today which are unwilling participants of the dollar area, we really only have to worry about a figure of seven or eight countries. Consequently, I would not exclude under present conditions a partial asset-settlement system as a transitional device, since the EPU, as we all know, was itself a transitional arrangement.

SCITOVSKY: In regard to Randall Hinshaw's observation, I am aware that it is possible to work out an agreement for symmetrical asset settlement and official intervention. My argument for a wider use of the SDR is that there is every evidence of a tremendous private demand for international liquidity. This demand has aggravated our international monetary problems, and I have the strong feeling that these problems would be reduced in scope if SDRs could be held by individuals, corporations, and commercial banks.

WALLICH: My comment concerns Mr. Schleiminger's observations about convertibility. There are two ways of approaching this subject. There is the U. S. proposal to have full convertibility, but to hedge the privilege in such a way that a country never becomes seriously embarrassed. The hedge takes the form of prescribed adjustments in exchange rates; the country that loses reserves devalues at some point, the country that gains reserves must revalue. The countries discussing this matter in the Committee of Twenty, from what I know, do not object to the U. S. proposal of full convertibility. They object to the use of reserves as the indicator and trigger of exchange-rate movements, and they give excellent reasons, as anybody can, why such a trigger is not ideal. But the reason for reserve changes as a trigger is not because the United States thought it was ideal, but because, without such protection, the United States could not possibly accept a commitment of 100 percent convertibility.

If the world is not going to accept this form of trigger, I think we have to think seriously of the other way of limiting convertibility, the way proposed by Mr. Schleiminger— namely, some form of partial asset settlement. Mr.

Schleiminger proposes that such a partial-convertibility system should apply to all transactions, as under the EPU, but I think a better system would be to limit 100 percent convertibility to current-account transactions. This would seem to me a very logical division, particularly in an age when the balance of payments is dominated by a slopping around of speculative short-term capital movements.

GORDON K. DOUGLASS: I would like to go back to Peter Kenen's question: How do we get there from here? In his opening remarks yesterday, Robert Solomon indicated that most countries want to revise the system in which all countries, including most especially the United States, finance their deficits. It almost goes without saying that the American authorities are lukewarm about any reform which would remove the dollar as a means of settlement—at least as long as American reserves remain low and dollar liabilities remain high. But if a way could be found to boost reserves and reduce the dollar overhang, surely a trustworthy pledge by the American authorities could be made more negotiable.

The most feasible way to get there from here, it seems to me, is to find a set of effective exchange rates which will permit the United States to run a basic surplus for several years and to work out an arrangement which would permit the United States to receive SDRs or other nondollar assets when in surplus. I see few other ways to rebuild U. S. reserves. A return to a pure gold standard at a higher gold price surely is not the answer; this would redistribute reserve assets quite arbitrarily. I also doubt that the implementation of various proposals for quick consolidation of dollar overhang is feasible. Some of these proposals would reduce reserves, others would be likely to depress the growth rate of reserves, and still others would be regarded politically, I suspect, as a grossly discriminatory gift to the United States.

The main problem is for the United States to achieve a sustained basic surplus in its balance of payments. If such a surplus were achieved, many countries would of course be attracted to paying their debts with officially held dollars rather than other reserve assets, with the result that the gain to U. S. reserve assets might be small. To deal with this problem, some way would need to be found—perhaps through a special arrangement with the Fund—to allow the United States to purchase reserve assets with its own currency whenever the annual addition to its reserves would otherwise fall short of its payments surplus. If new reserve needs could be met mainly by internationally created reserve assets, such as SDRs, the SDR portion of world reserves might rise to perhaps two-thirds of the total by as early as 1980. Assuming a sustained U. S. payments surplus, the restoration of dollar convertibility under such conditions would appear to be feasible.

Chairman THORP: Thank you; we'll all check on you in 1980. One minute to Professor Schmidt.

WILSON E. SCHMIDT: Just to emphasize what Gordon Douglass has just said, I picked out what I thought was a key issue in the recent press conference of Jeremy Morse, Chairman of the Deputies of the Committee of Twenty. "Question: May I ask you, Mr. Chairman, whether you think that the other countries of the world are willing to give the United States the type of adjustment that it needs to make the dollar convertible? Mr. Morse: I don't know whether they are, but that's the essence of reform. If they are, well, then, we shall have a nice reform; if they're not, then we shall have something else."

KENEN: Let me make a brief comment on the observations of Wilson Schmidt and Gordon Douglass. First of all, Jeremy Morse's succinct statement, to which Wilson referred, raises two separate issues. One is whether we can have asset settlements without a decent adjustment mechanism. The answer is no. But there is an additional requirement: we must have adequate reserves to start with. Morse is responding implicitly with one answer to two questions: First, will we get an adjustment mechanism that will allow the United States to have convertibility if its reserves are already adequate? Second, will we get an adjustment mechanism that will allow the United States to earn adequate reserves? Now I'm not sure whether one should throw the task of earning reserves onto the new adjustment mechanism. The burden one would impose on the new mechanism by accommodating it to the transitional needs of the United States would so warp the new rules of the game as to make them asymmetrical.

Professor Douglass's assumption of a transition period, ending perhaps in 1980, may be at issue here. But would a promise of convertibility delayed to 1980 buy us in the interim an agreement on the other dimensions of reform? I am afraid that a promise so long deferred and so heavily discounted will be of very little use in the negotiating process. I am perhaps more skeptical than Professor Douglass about the willingness of other countries to allow the United States to run the payments surpluses necessary to acquire adequate reserves. If there were agreement on that issue, then surely technical devices could be worked out to deal directly with, or to sidestep, the consolidation question and the question of the form in which the United States would receive the proceeds of its surpluses. The basic question is whether there is a political and economic will to permit the necessary improvement in the U. S. balance of payments—not only to end the present deficit, but also to acquire several billion dollars of reserves in a brief period of time. After all, 1980 is only seven years away.

RICHARD N. COOPER: I would like to pick up some themes introduced by Peter Kenen and Tibor Scitovsky and to offer what I think is a constructive suggestion. Let me say first of all that the suggestion by Scitovsky to make the SDR a private as well as a public international currency seems to me pretty far off, whatever one may think of its desirability. Here I agree with Frank Southard. To get private markets to accept and deal in SDRs on the kind of scale and with the kind of flexibility necessary to keep the world economy going smoothly is something that will take many years.

The desire for symmetry is really an esthetic desire and, as an esthetic norm, is something to be approached but never fully attained. There is a fundamental asymmetry in the world which we just can't ignore, and that is the size of the United States. There is no way around it; the size of the United States gives the U. S. dollar a status in the world that is simply not the same as the status of the Guatemalan quetzal, for example. We see this fact in the very extensive private holdings of dollar balances around the world.

This is the subject I want to raise now, because it seems to me that talk of dollar consolidation, convertibility, and adjustment without taking into account the large private balances is useless as a basis for a satisfactory and durable monetary reform. Even if all of the official balances were swept away, the United States—even with an adequate adjustment mechanism—could not accept a convertibility obligation because of the many billions of dollars in private holdings around the world. These could flood foreign central banks at any time, regardless of the state of the U. S. balance of payments. If the United States had a convertibility obligation, it would be obliged to convert into primary reserve assets all those dollar flows to foreign central banks, unless one were to adopt a Wallich-type solution that confines convertibility to dollars arising from current-account deficits.

All of this suggests to me that we need some way to handle the problem of movements of large private balances from one currency into another. We should strive for a system which is robust against a variety of contingencies. Now there is a classical way of doing this, and indeed it gave rise to modern central banking. The classical solution was the creation of a lender of last resort. We do not have an international lender of last resort at the present time. We have the International Monetary Fund, with a capacity to lend—under conditions that vary from not very onerous to quite onerous—amounts which are negligible in relation to the magnitude of the problem as it now presents itself. I would suggest, therefore, that we should establish, in addition to the present General Account and the SDR Account of the Fund, a third account which would have the capacity to lend to countries—here I'm thinking particularly of the United States, because that is where the big problem lies— in case of a very large conversion of private balances into official balances. There is no technical reason why this couldn't be done. The Fund could lend in the form of SDRs whenever there were massive movements of funds, and it could lend, in principle, without limit.

How would such a facility tie in with the adjustment process? I would envisage matters working in the following way. If there were large movements of funds—and by large I have in mind the kind of movements that we have had recently, $2 billion in a single day, $6 billion in a week, though they may be even bigger in the future—the Fund, in a convertible world, would lend without hesitation to cover that kind of movement. Any questions would be asked after things had settled down—and simply for the purpose of determining how the situation should be tidied up. If the movement were promptly reversed, then the Fund would be repaid within a short period of a few months. If the shift in private portfolios were of a more durable nature, then it should trigger adjustment, and one could imagine funding this IMF lending on a fixed amortization schedule covering a period of many years.

Thus if we are to talk meaningfully about a reformed system that involves convertibility, we must provide some mechanism to handle large-scale movements of private dollar holdings. If that necessary condition were met, then the question of official dollar balances really becomes a secondary issue; to use Professor Kenen's language, one could sidestep that issue because, if one chose, official dollar balances could be handled in exactly the same way. I foresee resistance to compulsory consolidation of official dollar balances, and since we need a mechanism in any case to handle private dollar balances, compulsory consolidation of official balances would be unnecessary. The same mechanism could handle shifts both in official portfolios and in private portfolios.

SOLOMON: I think what Dick Cooper has proposed deserves careful consideration, and I am not going to quarrel with his broad proposition. I do, however, have one comment. Dick gave the impression that the facility he suggested would be needed only by the United States. I am surprised at Dick, who is usually so forward-looking; he's sitting here fighting the last war. I can well imagine a situation in the not so distant future when there is an expectation that the dollar will be revalued upward. Just think of the flow of private funds into the dollar at such a time! I can well imagine that Dick's facility would then be needed, not by the United States, but by many other countries.

Chairman THORP: One minute to Professor Frank.

ISAIAH FRANK: My comment concerns Peter Kenen's observations on transitional arrangements, but I think it is equally pertinent to what Dick Cooper has just said. Whether we are talking about private dollar balances or official dollar balances, the only way any amortization of either overhang can be accomplished is for the United States to run a surplus on current account. This is the key problem; the United States would not be able to reduce the dollar overhang in any of the ways suggested unless Japan and the Europeans permit it to run a current-account surplus.

Stating the matter in this way raises the possibility of a different kind of link proposal. In building up large dollar liabilities, the United States, as we all know, has drawn real resources from the rest of the world. But the rich countries don't really want to be paid back; they don't want to be placed in a position of current-account deficit. Instead of repaying the rich countries, why couldn't an arrangement be worked out in which the International Monetary Fund would dole out installments of SDRs to the developing countries to be used

for purchases from the United States, which would then use
the SDRs to amortize the dollar overhang? This seems to
me a very promising approach, since the dollar overhang can
be reduced only if some countries run a current-account
deficit. The obvious candidates are the developing countries,
which need real resources from the rest of the world. This
use of SDRs would be entirely separate from the more widely
discussed link between development assistance and the creation of new reserve assets to meet the world's liquidity needs.

VI. THE DESIGN OF REFORM: OTHER VIEWS

*Gottfried Haberler and
Members of the Conference*

Chairman THORP: This afternoon, we will continue our exploration of this broad terrain concerned with the structure of reform. Our first speaker is Professor Haberler.

GOTTFRIED HABERLER: When I ask myself what most members here seem to agree on, it is a negative proposition—namely, that the prevailing system, the dollar standard, is not acceptable. Lord Robbins expressed that view, and almost everybody else appears to have started from that assumption.

When we come to positive matters, we are clearly far from agreement. Some want to go back to gold, others want to have the SDR take over the international role of the dollar, and still others want floating exchange rates. Of course, nobody really wants all currencies to float against all others; that is just a straw man put up by some of the defenders of fixed exchange rates. What is recommended is that certain currency blocs should float against other blocs.

But the fact of life is that we are still on a dollar standard—and more so than ever in the last few years. In a certain sense, the dollar standard is more secure than it ever was, for the simple reason that the volume of official liquid dollar holdings now is greater than ever, having grown to $70 billion. The larger these balances, the more difficult it is to get rid of them or to consolidate them, so I suggest that the only realistic assumption is that this system will continue for a considerable period. It is almost inconceivable that within a short period—say, within the next few years—anything comprehensive in the way of a complete restructuring of the international monetary system will come about.

In the meantime, the world has to go on, and world trade will doubtless keep on growing. Fortunately, in spite of all our crises, things have gone fairly well, so instead of only considering what eventually we would want to put in place of the present system, we should consider whether it might not be possible to make the present system work a little better — to make the dollar standard, with which we are stuck for some time, a little more acceptable.

In this connection, let me make one or two suggestions. Of course, the greatest contribution the United States could make to improve the working of the system would be to slow down its inflation. So long as the world is on a dollar standard in the sense that the majority of countries peg their currencies to the dollar, the United States really sets the pace for world inflation. Other countries either go along with this situation or, if they don't want to do that, they have to appreciate or to let their currencies float upward. Of course, some countries inflate at a greater rate than the United States; they have to devalue or to let their currencies float downward.

But the statement that the pace of world inflation is set by the United States has to be qualified. It is strictly true if we define inflation in terms of the price level of internationally traded goods. If, however, we define inflation in the more usual sense of the rise in the consumer price index, then my proposition is not quite accurate. This can best be illustrated by the case of Japan. In terms of the consumer price index, Japan has had a much higher rate of inflation than the United States. Yet this fact has not prevented Japan from having a tremendous export surplus both in general and with the United States. The reason is that export prices in Japan and in the United States behave in a different way. If we look at Japanese export prices, they have risen much less rapidly than Japanese consumer prices, or, to express the matter slightly differently, the wholesale price level in Japan has risen much less than the consumer price index. The reason is that, in a rapidly growing country where productivity and standards of living are rising fast, consumer prices always rise faster than wholesale prices, because wages rise and, therefore, services become more expensive. Services, as we all know, loom very large in the consumer price index. In the United States, the situation is reversed; export prices have risen more rapidly than consumer prices.

So we have this paradox that the United States sets the pace of world inflation, even though some countries inflate more in terms of consumer prices and still have an export surplus. In other words, the United States sets the pace of inflation, but with a coefficient that is different for different countries, so that troubles can arise even if the United States has less inflation than other countries.

What I want to suggest now is this: keeping in mind that U. S. inflation may become worse than it is right now and that, even if it does not become worse, some countries may accumulate dollars which they don't want, we could make that situation more acceptable and more equitable by offering a purchasing-power guarantee for official foreign dollar holdings. From a purely economic standpoint, I believe that a purchasing-power guarantee in terms, say, of internationally traded goods at the U. S. wholesale price level, would be a most constructive improvement in the present system.

Understandably, American policy makers have not made this proposal. They don't like the idea because they are afraid that it would cost an immense amount of money. In my opinion, such a guarantee would not cost a great deal of money, because the interest rate on such guaranteed balances clearly could be much lower than on unguaranteed balances. The facility would be voluntary; official holders would have the option either of investing in treasury obligations of the present type at high rates of interest or of investing in obligations with a purchasing-power guarantee at low rates of interest. I haven't worked out the matter in detail, but a very rough calculation would suggest that the purchasing-power guarantee would cost the U. S. Treasury very little.

This is only one suggestion. The main thrust of my argument is that we should pay more attention to transitional improvements. This is a transitional period, but experience tells us that transitional periods and provisional arrangements sometimes last for a long time. We will be a little closer to reality if we spend more time on these so-called transitional arrangements than if we talk only about utopian solutions which, if they ever come at all, will come only in the distant future.

Chairman THORP: One minute to the Moderator.

Lord ROBBINS: I won't take one minute; I only want to ask Gottfried how he would define the limits of this privilege. To whom would it be extended? From whom would it be denied? I want to know the class of persons owning dollars who would enjoy the privilege of the guarantee.

HABERLER: Under my proposal, official dollar holders would have the choice either of investing as presently in the market at the current interest rate or of obtaining a purchasing-power guarantee on Treasury bonds at a lower interest rate.

Lord ROBBINS: And this would be limited to official holders?

HABERLER: Oh, yes, certainly; it would be only for official dollar holders.

C. DILLON GLENDINNING: I wonder if I might make a comment on Professor Haberler's proposal. I suspect that any such purchasing-power guarantee, presumably limited to dollar balances held by official institutions, could easily become an open-ended guarantee for most foreign-held dollar balances. What are foreign private balances today can become official balances tomorrow, and what are U. S. domestic bank deposits today can become deposits with foreign banks tomorrow. Short of comprehensive exchange controls, I can think of no mechanism which would assure that such a guarantee would be limited to some holders of dollars and not to others, and I fear that the guarantee might have a disastrous effect both on the level of foreign dollar balances and on their distribution as between official and private holders.

HABERLER: But we discriminate between official and private dollar holders all the time. Until August 1971, official dollar balances were convertible into U. S. gold, and private dollar balances have not enjoyed that privilege since 1933. I don't see any difficulty with respect to the purchasing-power guarantee in this connection. Of course, we know that enormous quantities of dollars are held privately and that they can at any time pass into official hands. This is part of the present system, but that has not made the system unworkable. If my proposal were accepted, the system would go on as it does now. There would be periods when private holdings moved to the official sector and then would be entitled to a purchasing-power guarantee. But this would not provide the private holder with an additional inducement to get rid of his dollars, as the guarantee would not apply to him in any case.

PETER B. KENEN: Without necessarily endorsing Professor Haberler's suggestion, I see no difficulty in distinguishing who is eligible for the guarantee and who is not. The holder who presents the asset for redemption could be made to identify himself as an official holder in order to qualify for the purchasing-power guarantee.

RICHARD N. COOPER: Taking up exactly the same point from a somewhat different angle, I would like to ask Gottfried what objection he sees to an alternative solution to this problem—namely, to extend the purchasing-power guarantee to all holders. The case has been made elsewhere that, in an inflationary environment, private citizens should have the option of purchasing-power guaranteed government securities, and I would like to hear Gottfried's reaction to this proposal.

HABERLER: I would agree that, in an inflationary setting, there is a great deal to be said for extending the purchasing-power guarantee to private savers. If we go on inflating as we have in the past, I think that sooner or later we will have to go in that direction, as the Brazilians have already.

Lord ROBBINS: May I say that when such proposals have been ventilated in Great Britain, I have always been met with the answer that no self-respecting government is prepared to legislate on the assumption of its own future incompetence.

Chairman THORP: I think we have chased this particular rabbit as far as we should. The next speaker is Fritz Machlup.

FRITZ MACHLUP: Mr. Chairman, on your advice I am changing the subject slightly, and would like to return to the question of the numeraire. I first want to register a protest against economic illiteracy. The word "numeraire" was first used by Walras for exactly the opposite purpose for which it is now being used—namely, to refer to something that is neither a store of value nor a medium of exchange. If we apply the term now to something that is employed as a medium of exchange or a store of value or both, we are using the term in a meaning entirely different from the traditional one. But I shall go along with what is now becoming majority usage, though less ambiguous terms might be "common denominator" or "unit of account."

In principle, a numeraire does not have to be a commodity; it does not have to be a store of value; it does not have to be a standard of value for goods; it does not have to be a unit of account in private transactions; it does not have to be an intervention asset, a settlement asset, or a conversion asset—it can be something completely different from all of these things. It can be simply an abstract unit, in relation to which various countries establish a parity or central rate for their currencies. It does not have to be an asset or a liability; it could be a unit like a kilometer or a meter. One could say that one currency unit is two meters and another is four meters; we would then know exactly the ratio between the two. To be clear on this is analytically helpful, and it certainly is useful pedagogically to put students through this mental exercise so they will not confuse matters that are logically separate and distinct.

But now let's come down to earth. We may doubt that practical bankers can think well enough in abstract terms to determine par values in such abstract units as meters, kilometers, or units of account. They may find it difficult to think in terms other than of some asset; indeed, many have been shuddering when the SDR, the novel kind of reserve asset, was nominated for the role of numeraire. Nevertheless, evolution in this direction seems to be most likely; the cognoscenti see it in the cards. A Fund unit of account will probably become the numeraire—whether it is called the SDR, which I consider a rather unimaginative name, or something else.

Now what does it mean if countries actually decide to establish par values in terms of the SDR? At the present time, the SDR is defined as equivalent to a fixed quantity of gold; not much would be gained by stating par values in terms of SDRs as long as this situation exists. But it stands to reason that, in the course of broad reforms of the international monetary system, this definition of the SDR will be changed. In that case, I can visualize the agonies of lawyers who cannot imagine anything that is not defined in terms of something else. Many lawyers have a hard time imagining a unit that is no more than a unit. We may have to refer them to the poetry of Gertrude Stein: a unit is a unit is a unit.

ROBERT A. MUNDELL: Just a comment on the numeraire. When we talk about the numeraire problem, I think we should restrict the term to the very correct use of it that Fritz Machlup outlined at the beginning and not assign it to an asset that is being held. We should be linguistically conservative in this regard.

The SDR has already slipped into a kind of usage as a unit of account. According to the February 12th press report of the Secretary of the Treasury on the recent dollar devaluation, "the President is requesting that the Congress authorize a further realignment of exchange rates. This objective will be sought by a formal 10 percent reduction in the par value of the dollar from .92106 SDR to the dollar to .82895 SDR to the dollar." The Secretary then states that he would "like to stress that this technical change has no practical significance."

I would argue on the contrary that this change may have vast and far-reaching significance, because it raises the question of the price of the SDR in terms of gold and the fixity of that relationship. If the Fund were to change the SDR price of gold, this would be a fundamental change in the entire monetary system. This is not a technical issue; it is a highly important matter concerning the future of the international monetary structure. I would not want to press any officials to comment on this issue at the present time, although it would be great if Mr. Southard could say something about it.

Chairman THORP: He has already signaled his willingness to comment. Frank, you have the floor.

FRANK A. SOUTHARD, JR.: Let me make a very harmless comment that won't, I'm afraid, satisfy Bob. At the press conference that the Secretary of the Treasury had last Monday night, the only way he could get the newspaper men to understand what had happened was to tell them that the devaluation meant $42.22 per ounce of gold. I would not want to argue with Bob that the definition of the dollar in terms of SDRs is not a potentially important step, although, as a minor legal matter, the Articles of Agreement would have to be changed before the Fund could officially accept a par value expressed in terms other than gold. That does not prevent the Fund from accepting— I believe I'm right on this—a sort of double barreled submission in terms of both gold and the SDR.

Chairman THORP: The Chairman would like to give himself a few seconds to ask a question of Fritz Machlup. Isn't the price of gold as we fix it so artificial that a unit of gold becomes a numeraire in practical terms—the basis on which we work out ratios between currencies?

MACHLUP: It could be so if people were agreed that the so-called official price of gold—that figure which was $35, then $38, and is now $42.22 per ounce—would never have any connection with the market price of gold. Only then could the fictitious value of monetary gold play exactly the role the Chairman has proposed. But I am afraid that the general public, the lawyers, and the journalists would not grasp it— except, of course, those lawyers and journalists who have Ph.D. degrees in economics. They would always say, "This

$42.22 is an unrealistic price; yesterday the real price was $72.80 and, therefore, we should adjust the official price."
I am afraid that there would be endless bickering and that the authorities would have a hard time making it understood that this so-called official price of gold was merely a numeraire, or common denominator, and nothing else.

Chairman THORP: There was a foreign country in which, because of certain religious beliefs combined with the need for food, the name of a particular animal was changed in order to get it off the prohibition list in the country's dietary laws. Perhaps we need to distinguish between private gold and official gold by deciding that one of them is chemically different from the other.

ROBERT SOLOMON: I'm afraid I must report that Bob Mundell has been parodying the Secretary of the Treasury.

MUNDELL: That was a quotation.

SOLOMON: I know, but let me read more of it to you. You are the last person who should be parodying anybody, Mr. Mundell. It is true, as you indicated, that the statement contains the following words: "The par value of the dollar is reduced 10 percent from .92106 SDR to the dollar to .82895 SDR to the dollar." But immediately following this sentence is a sentence commencing a new paragraph which reads as follows: "All of this action will under the existing Articles of Agreement of the IMF result in a change in the official relationship of the dollar to gold. I should like to stress that this technical change has no practical significance." So what the Secretary of the Treasury was saying is somewhat more on the lines of what Fritz was saying—that gold is now a numeraire in the sense in which Fritz and Bob agree. But the Secretary did not say that the change in defining the dollar in terms of SDRs is of no practical significance.

LEONARD S. SILK: I don't know whether the subject is so scholastic that one shouldn't stay with it any longer, but, for what it's worth, my own reading of the Secretary's statement—in which two things that are allegedly identical are defined so that one of them has practical significance and the other does not—is as follows: The changed relationship to the SDR is taken to indicate the changed par-value relationship between the dollar and other currencies. The changed relationship to gold has no practical significance because it is assumed that governments will behave themselves and not ask for anything at the new price.

MUNDELL: May I say something here? I had no intention of misleading. But I would like to point out to Robert Solomon that I don't believe the Secretary of the Treasury really means that an increase in the value of gold reserves to all official holders, amounting to several billion dollars, has no practical significance.

Chairman THORP: The Chairman rules that the correct interpretation of the statement of the Secretary of the Treasury cannot be determined in his absence and that we have now had enough speculation about it.

MUNDELL: Well, Mr. Chairman, this issue of the numeraire seems to me an extremely important matter. We have obviously struck a nerve center at this point and, in view of the very expert group that we have here at this table, we should not evade this issue but should explicitly discuss the question of whether the SDR should be the pivot point for currency parities or whether we should retain gold for this purpose. We should also discuss whether the SDR should continue to be defined in terms of gold and, if so, whether the present parity in terms of gold should be retained.

I am not talking simply about my own views on these matters; I would like personally to know the views of the other members. Should we move in the direction of making the SDR over the long run into a true world currency? Of course, John Exter would not like that, but many people are thinking in these terms. Should we adopt a system that has a numeraire in the strict sense defined by Fritz Machlup, in which the SDR is, in effect, a ghost of gold rather than an asset that is convertible into gold? Should we let this embryo of a world money begin to take on its own significance?

On another matter, the recent 11 percent increase in the dollar price of gold increases the reserves of gold-holding countries to that extent. This is clearly a matter which should be taken into account in deciding future allocations of SDRs.

SOLOMON: On that question, I do not want to pick on my friend across the table . . .

Chairman THORP: Why not?

SOLOMON: Well, I agree with Bob Mundell that the issues he has raised certainly deserve discussion, but let me correct one statement he made. He said that the decision of the United States to devalue and therefore to raise the official price of gold by 11 percent increases the reserves of gold-holding countries. Only the <u>dollar</u> value of reserves, Robert. The

D-mark value of gold reserves has not changed, and the yen value of gold reserves has gone down in the past week. I would guess that the average currency value of gold remains about the same. In a world which may be less dollar-centered in the future—if Professor Haberler will permit me to imagine that— we should not think only of the dollar value of international monetary reserves.

ROBERT TRIFFIN: I agree with Bob Mundell about the importance of the shift to the SDR as a numeraire. But if we move in this direction, we have to consider what meaning remains to the price of gold.

There are all kinds of possible meanings. One is simply the bookkeeping price of gold, and that can vary from central bank to central bank. A central bank for a long time may keep the value of gold in its books at cost; at some point, it may revalue the gold at some other price. Then there is another— and rather absurd—meaning in which one can speak about the price at which central banks now abstain from either buying or selling gold, whether that price is $35, $38, or $42.22.

There is a third question: Do we expect central banks to sit on their gold forever and not to have any transactions in gold, or do we expect them at some stage to resume transactions in gold? If so, at what price? Should there be a new fixed price, or should there simply be the free-market price of gold as a commodity?

Finally, there is the question of whether central banks should have dealings with the private market and, if so, whether the rules for sales by central banks to the market should be the same as the rules for purchases by central banks from the market. The rules might well be different, because the issues are very different—although these issues were confused, for reasons I have never quite understood, in the Washington agreement of March 1968 establishing the two-tier system.

SOUTHARD: One small point. I agree on the whole with what Bob Triffin has said. The entire question of the status of gold as a central bank asset and of the March 1968 agreement is a wide-open issue. I don't think it is any secret that the U. S. government has come to a view of the 1968 agreement on gold which is very different from its view at the time the agreement was negotiated. And there are even rumors that central banks which have a lot of gold, and which are very troubled at this gold being frozen, are thinking of the possibility of having transactions among themselves at or near the free-market price. So we obviously have some very real questions of conflict within the system.

MACHLUP: I think we should take up for a moment the suggestion of Bob Mundell and ask ourselves whether we find transferring the role of numeraire from gold to the SDR a desirable change. That depends very much, it seems to me, on our forecast of what will happen to supply and demand in the gold market. In the long run, I think that the two tiers for transactions in gold will not endure. If we believe that there will be no great stability in the free-market price for gold, if we believe that there may be drastic and perhaps whimsical changes in supply—for example, withholding part of current production from the market—or that there may be drastic changes in demand of a speculative character, then I believe it would be wiser to liberate the international monetary system from this funny business of an official price, or book value, of gold. But if we do that, and if we still adhere to any kind of par-value system, we must find something else in which to express these par values. Whether we call the unit an SDR or something else really does not make much difference. On the whole, I believe it is desirable to switch from gold to something else as the unit for determining parities. As the late Albert Hahn used to say, a slide rule does not have to be made of gold.

GUENTHER SCHLEIMINGER: In his remarks about the numeraire, Professor Mundell has mentioned the possibility of separating the SDR from gold. It seems to me that only such a numeraire would make sense. Otherwise, we are making only a cosmetic change. But if we separate the SDR from a tie to gold, are people prepared and willing to live with this kind of abstraction, in which, as Fritz Machlup pointed out, an SDR equals an SDR? There are proposals which would link the SDR as a numeraire to an index of currency values in order to eliminate any devaluation bias in the system. I am rather irritated by this kind of numeraire in terms of an index, and I would be interested in the views of others around this table.

Chairman THORP: The Chairman finds it rather extraordinary that we put the emphasis we do on gold as some kind of source of value at a time when we cannot deal in it and when the value is arbitrarily fixed by action of Congress. What is there about gold that gives it this attractiveness in such an artificial setting?

SOLOMON: Let me say a word or two in answer to the question you have raised.

You asked why there is this interest in gold. Well, there is no urgent immediate problem or action in the international monetary field that is being held up because of uncertainty about the future role of gold. But in the longer run, and in the context of reform—which, after all, is what we are discussing—we shall have to settle somehow the role to be played by gold. Though of less importance than in the past, gold happens to constitute the great bulk of the reserves of the United States and of many other countries. It is of great importance to these countries what the future role of gold will be—particularly the United States, whose reserves are mainly in the form of gold.

But for most countries, there is no urgency about ending the so-called immobilization of gold. One has to do it in the long run, but at the moment there is no great pressure. I can think of no foreign country that has a prospective payments deficit which doesn't have a rather healthy cushion of dollars to finance such a deficit before it gets down to its gold reserves; and I would guess that, whatever is done about the future role of gold, countries will tend in the years immediately ahead to use foreign exchange before they use gold.

SILK: It seems to me that there are really two things in this world called gold as long as we have the two-tier system. At the bottom of the two tiers, we have what we can call Gold 1, postmarked 1968, which is really a nonexistent form of gold; it is actually an SDR. Secretary Shultz's statement reflected this state of affairs, and to the extent that anyone is interested in Gold 1, he is really interested in the SDR price. Under the two-tier system, countries are, in effect, on an SDR numeraire. If that agreement breaks down, with central banks settling at the free-market price of gold—settling in Gold 2—this of course creates problems for an SDR numeraire. So one issue is whether central banks should take the pledge to stick to Gold 1 rather than to bolt to Gold 2.

MACHLUP: Mr. Chairman, I submit that the question of the future role of gold as a reserve asset has to be completely separated from the question of the numeraire. Indeed, I think some great friends of gold, believers in the future role of gold as a reserve asset, are now willing to give up the official price of monetary gold and to allow countries to deal on the private market or at least to have transactions among themselves at the free-market price. If that is the case, it would clearly be better to assign the numeraire function to something else, such as the SDR.

I did not quite understand why the Chairman was so astonished that gold is still important in the minds of some people. After all, we have John Exter in our midst and, if you will pardon the pun, there are many "External" economists in the world, including some central bank officials. If our thinking about reform is to be realistic, we have to recognize this sentiment.

Chairman THORP: Dick Cooper has asked for the floor.

RICHARD N. COOPER: I would like to give one person's view on a question that Bob Mundell put earlier—whether we should or should not use the SDR as a standard, and I would like to offer a solution to the problem of official gold, a solution which at the present moment would doubtless be unacceptable to central banks, but which, I dare to hope, might become acceptable at a later date.

I think we should move to the SDR as a standard, with all the changes in the IMF Articles of Agreement that this will require. Whether we do that on some sort of index basis, along the lines of proposals to which Mr. Schleiminger has referred, is a secondary issue, and depends on how people feel at the time. It is easy to imagine doing it that way, but it is also easy to imagine doing it without linking the SDR to a market basket of currencies. The only differences between the two arrangements concern the amount of SDRs that would have to be created at the time of currency devaluations, the technical method of carrying out devaluations (a market-basket approach would require changes in all par values to accommodate a change in any one par value), and—perhaps most important—the real burden of external debt denominated in SDRs.

Leonard Silk is quite right in pointing out that the existing monetary gold, which he calls Gold 1 and which I call "blue gold," is really the SDR in disguise. One possible solution to the official gold problem would be to convert all of the gold that central banks now hold into a special issue of SDRs. By hiring a skillful marketeer, the IMF could then feed the gold into the market at a rate that did not drive the price down too rapidly, thereby earning substantial capital gains on the gold, which could then be used for some form of foreign aid.

Many of the objections which central bankers have made with respect to other "link" proposals do not apply to this particular form of aid. In particular, the sale of an official asset to the private market extracts resources from the general public which could be transferred to the less developed countries. Unlike SDR creation, gold sales represent a genuine fiscal operation.

I recognize that this proposal is not likely to recommend itself to central bankers who still have a lingering suspicion that the international monetary system may end up being a gold standard after all and that they therefore must hedge the future by continuing to hold on to their gold. But my own feeling is that we should move as rapidly as we can to an SDR system, at the same time using the existing official gold in an internationally constructive way.

ROY BLOUGH: My thinking about what to do with official gold has not gone as far as Dick Cooper's, but it seems to me that one of the best arguments against raising the official price of gold is that when you raise it even a little bit, the speculative market is so stimulated by that rise that the free-market price tends to zoom upward, putting more and more pressure on the official price.

That is precisely what has already happened. The official price has gone from $35 to $38, and now to $42.22 an ounce. Far from reducing speculation, these changes have greatly increased it. There are some who would like the official price raised to the free-market price, but the best thing in my judgment would be to adopt the SDR as the numeraire and announce that, from now on, the IMF will include in world reserves the number of ounces held in the form of gold, but will put no value on them. Another possibility would be for central banks to sell their gold to the IMF and let SDRs take its place.

HABERLER: It seems to me that the really important question is the role of gold, SDRs, dollars, or anything else as a reserve rather than as a pure numeraire. This matter of the numeraire seems to me a rather unimportant question. The reserve function, on the other hand, is extremely important and, from a rational standpoint, everything is to be said for replacing gold with SDRs. This is a case where you can have your cake and eat it too. It is the same case that Adam

Smith described when he said that replacing gold with paper money is like building roads in the air instead of using up valuable space on earth. From a purely rational standpoint, replacing gold with SDRs is very sensible, but, practically speaking, I'm afraid that it is out of the question, because there are many countries in the world—France, for example, but also many others—which are so wedded to gold that they would never agree to any such proposal. In time, they may be educated to a different outlook, but it will be a very long time.

HENRY C. WALLICH: Now that the United States has devalued against gold and the SDR, there is a profit for countries which peg to the dollar, and therefore I doubt that anything can be done about gold before everybody has cashed in on this profit. And since countries will figure that this kind of thing may repeat itself, I doubt very much that we can persuade countries to relinquish their gold. Apart from profit hopes, there is the fear of an ultimate breakdown of any paper system, including the SDR system. If there were such a breakdown, countries would be obliged to buy back gold, perhaps at much higher prices. So I think the logic of the situation is to stress the SDR in every way conceivable, just as Secretary Shultz did in his statement, and to keep hammering away at phasing out gold slowly, but not to make a very great issue of it and to let events take their course.

COOPER: My comments refer to remarks just made by Gottfried Haberler and Henry Wallich. In order for my proposal to work, it would not be necessary to get every country to agree. If France, for example, did not wish to participate, it could hold on to its gold. All that would be necessary would be to get a consensus among a considerable number of countries. Once the amount of monetary gold goes down from the present forty tons to something like twenty tons or ten tons, gold is simply out of the running as a monetary standard.

I did not fully understand Henry Wallich's point about foregone profit; measured in dollars or in local currency pegged on the dollar, there would be no greater profit on official gold than there would be on SDRs following a devaluation of the dollar. I believe the only serious objection to my proposal is the second one Henry mentioned—the lingering fear of a breakdown of a paper standard.

WALLICH: Dick has raised a very interesting point with the thought of profits on SDRs, because the writing up in value of a piece of paper is going to give people around the world some pause.

SOLOMON: I seldom disagree with Dick, but one of us is technically wrong on one point. If countries were given the opportunity to exchange gold for SDRs by the Fund, at what value relationship would this exchange take place. I presume that the exchange would not take place at the current free-market price for gold.

COOPER: That is correct.

SOLOMON: Well, I think it is rather unlikely that central banks would accept from the Fund a lower price for gold in terms of SDRs than they could get for that gold in the free market. They wouldn't sell.

COOPER: If your premise is correct, then you are right; they would never sell. But I would be happy to press the matter, because it would force central banks into admitting that they are, in fact, speculators. Most of the major countries now claim they already have an excess of reserves, even valuing gold at the official price. For them to refuse a straight exchange for SDRs in these circumstances would expose their hypocrisy. To allow them to exchange gold among themselves at the market price would just feed the inflation they profess to abhor.

MUNDELL: To talk at the present time about diminishing the role of gold, whether that would be a good thing or not, seems to me an academician's pipe dream until a viable alternative to gold is found. At a time when everyone is trying to find hedges against inflation, the movement toward gold is inevitable, and its rising price reflects that fact. It is no secret that some regional groupings are considering writing up the price at which they will privately trade gold among themselves. At the present time, gold has ceased to function as an international means of payment, because everybody wants to hoard rather than spend an asset which they know, or think they know, is undervalued. Now if a group, especially a group as important as the European Common Market, were to increase the price of gold for transactions among themselves, the implications for the whole international monetary system would be enormous, because that would move us toward a sporadic increase in the official price of gold, in much the way that such an increase occurred during the 1930s. If that were to occur, the state of the world we are talking about would be fundamentally different, and our policies should be adjusted to speed or hinder that end, depending on whether we approve or dislike its consequences.

Chairman THORP: I think we should let Frank Southard have the last word in this discussion.

SOUTHARD: If we are looking ahead to a new system, then I would agree completely with Bob Mundell that we don't need to worry about any inhibitions under the present statutes, but I think it is generally known that under the present Articles of the Fund, central banks can sell gold at the current free-market price but cannot buy it.

Now the gold agreement of March 1968 has no status under the Fund Articles. The Fund was never a party to it, and when, as has happened, a central bank has come to the Fund and said, "Look, we are badly in need of dollars, and we have some gold which we are willing to sell, but we certainly don't want to sell it at the official price," the Fund has told the central bank that, so far as the Fund is concerned, it could sell the gold in the free market. And some central banks have done so.

VII. TRADE ISSUES IN INTERNATIONAL MONETARY REFORM

*Isaiah Frank and
Members of the Conference*

Chairman THORP: The purists in our group have no difficulty in defining what is included in the phrase, "international monetary problems"—namely, those problems that relate to the machinery of foreign exchange and to adjustment in the balance of payments. Recently, at least in statements by the U. S. Administration, this definition has been substantially expanded in such a way that trade problems and investment problems are joined with purely monetary problems under the general heading of international monetary reform.

And, in our own discussions, these matters have from time to time attracted attention. The question is really how far one looks behind the numbers in the actual balance of payments to the forces which affect them. One could easily argue that the question of international demand and supply elasticities is not only a trade problem but also a monetary problem; and certainly when Sir Roy Harrod suggested that, if other measures failed, countries could or should resort to quantitative import restrictions, he was immediately bringing us into the trade field. To begin our discussion on the relation between trade policy and international monetary reform, I am calling on Isaiah Frank, who, because of his rich government experience in both areas, is in a particularly authoritative position to speak on this subject.

ISAIAH FRANK: I would like to begin by referring to a question that Lord Robbins posed yesterday in his opening remarks. After pointing out that we are concerned at this conference with problems of international monetary disorder, he asked whether we are dealing with something that really matters or merely with a subject which seems to be of intense interest to a small coterie of experts around the world.

I would submit that this is a question that should not be regarded as purely rhetorical. We have just been through an international monetary crisis, but it is not a crisis in the same sense as the Berlin crisis or the Cuban crisis or the Suez crisis, where the security of a state may have been at stake or where people may die or get injured. The recent crisis produced scarcely a ripple in terms of its effects on the ordinary person. And as a matter of fact, all the fears of economists regarding the profound political consequences on any Administration that would lead this country down the road to devaluation have been proven wrong. Congress doesn't seem to care; the matter seems beyond their ken, and they have accepted it.

Let me say at once that I do not share this lack of concern. If I may leap over what has been said about transitional arrangements, I think it is clear that most of us agree that any future system is going to be a convertible one—that we can no longer have a system in which the United States draws unlimited credit from others. This means that the United States will have to be prepared to convert dollars officially held abroad into primary assets. I also take it that we are all agreed that the United States should not incur large-scale unemployment in order to achieve a balanced payments position. Now without unlimited international credit as the United States has now, and without prompt changes in exchange rates, the only way this country can manage its external payments position is through various forms of control in the fields both of trade and of capital.

I think the point that Sir Roy Harrod made is very important, and should not be shrugged off. He asked: Why not import controls? Would it not be possible to devise import controls that would not have a seriously adverse effect on the United States in terms of economic efficiency or in terms of inflationary consequences, yet which at the same time would be effective in promoting external balance? That is looking at the matter from a rather parochial national point of view. But it seems to me that, apart from whatever the economic consequences may be, we have learned that import restrictions can have profound political consequences, yet the politics of the issues that are involved in international monetary reform have scarcely been mentioned here.

Even measures as limited as an increase in the tariff on carpets or glass can trigger reactions abroad which can undermine relations with other countries in a way which affects national security—not security in the sense of survival but in the sense that we would be confronted with an entirely different and more serious order of problems in managing our international affairs. I think it is no accident that, despite the fact that the General Agreement on Tariffs and Trade authorizes quantitative restrictions in cases of balance-of-payments difficulties, this authority has never been invoked to my knowledge by any of the major countries. It has never been invoked, not because it doesn't work, but because of an awareness on the part of those in authority of the political consequences of that kind of action. And all of us remember that, of the various measures instituted by the United States on August 15, 1971, the one which really got the dander up of other countries was the import surcharge. This caused far more tension abroad than the suspension of convertibility. So there is a political dimension here that we must very much bear in mind.

Now I would like to address myself briefly to the relationship between negotiations on trade and negotiations on monetary reform. In current Washington thinking about tariff negotiations, there is a fear that the conventional type of reciprocity may tend to produce an adverse effect on the U. S. trade balance. More specifically, there is a feeling that these elasticities we talked about operate perversely for the United States—that the price elasticity of the U. S. demand for imports, particularly of consumer goods, is high, whereas the price elasticity of foreign demand for U. S. exports, consisting heavily of agricultural products and high-technology goods, is low. If that is the case, the question becomes: Should we enter into new negotiations? Isn't there a very real danger that mutual reductions of tariffs would lead to a further deterioration in the U. S. balance of payments?

Well, the economist's answer, I suppose, would be that the purpose of trade negotiations is not to achieve any particular balance-of-payments result but rather to raise the level of trade and of real income. But that sort of benign view, it seems to me, can only be asserted on the assumption that, parallel with such negotiations, the world is making some progress in the reform of the international monetary system and particularly of the adjustment process, so that, whatever the effects of the negotiations on trade balances, the system will correct any tendency toward disequilibrium.

So in this sense, I think, there is much to the Administration view that trade and monetary reform have a kind of organic relationship. But there is a second relationship which I think is also worth mentioning; the first relationship explains why monetary reform is needed for further progress in trade negotiation, and the second explains why trade liberalization is important for monetary reform. In this second connection, the problem is that, the more countries rely on quantitative trade barriers, the more the adjustment of payments is focused on the narrowing range of economic activity that is free to respond to market forces. This can produce results which are sharper than are politically acceptable in some countries.

A clear example is the "common agricultural policy" of the European Economic Community. No change in exchange rates can affect the ability of the United States to sell agricultural products which are subject to the Community's "variable levy." Under such arrangements, improvements in the adjustment process, such as greater flexibility in exchange rates, are of no avail.

My final remarks are really speculative, because I have discovered that even people in the Administration are wondering what new authority in the trade field the Administration is going to request from Congress. But from reading the papers, I gather that one possibility being considered is the authority to impose uniform import surcharges across the board. One purpose of such a measure would be to deal with the transitional period before adjustment is achieved through "small and prompt" changes in exchange rates. The other authority apparently being considered as part of the new trade program is the authority to impose restrictions on individual products in cases of market disruption.

Well, my own view is that anyone who thinks that the United States is going to continue to take the lead in trade liberalization without dealing with the issue of market disruption is living in a dream world. There is absolutely no possibility of that, given the views both of the trade unions and of business. So whether we like them or not, we are going to have so-called "safeguard provisions." Our objective should be to subject such provisions to some kind of international criteria and surveillance in order to assure that any restrictions

thus imposed are in fact justified and are of brief duration—
that they disappear in a matter of three or, at most, four
years on a declining basis. In this way, safeguards can become a means by which we can liberalize trade rather than a
new instrument of protection.

And so, Mr. Chairman, although much of the semantics
and rhetoric of the Administration is nationalistic in tone and,
I must say, highly irritating to foreigners, I think there is
much to be said for some of the measures being considered.
I will end with that and with the conclusion that there is an
intimate relation between monetary reform and trade policy.

PETER B. KENEN: I would like to address myself to the
broader of the issues raised by Isaiah Frank. I was reading
this morning the draft of an article by Fred Hirsch, who made
a rather striking point. It is an obvious point when one thinks
about it, and I am sure that it has been made before, but it
needs repetition: We are in the process of building pieces of
an international system, not just an international monetary
system. This is a long-term effort, and has been going on
for a long time, starting, if you wish, with the Hague Conventions and the International Court of Arbitration. Because it is
a piecemeal process, because we have not established as a
first step a supranational police power with the right to discipline individual nations, we find ourselves in an awkward
position. Such sanctions as we can build into the separate
sequential parts of this international constitution—the sanctions we must incorporate in order to protect the system
against governmental misbehavior—have always to be applied
within the context of that particular part.

To be more specific, consider the sanctions we can devise
to protect the system against violations of the rules for trade
policy. Because those sanctions must relate to trade itself,
they have themselves to violate the rules of trade policy. What
can we do to discipline a nation that violates the rules of the
General Agreement on Tariffs and Trade? We can only erect
new trade barriers against the offending nation. Similarly, in
the monetary area, what sanctions can we devise? They have
to reside within the monetary system. This strange pattern
repeats itself monotonously, partly because the constituencies
in each case are separate, partly because one constituency
does not accept the jurisdiction of others, and partly because
of the sequential manner in which we are building the international system. The consequence, of course, is that the sub-

systems we build, being partial, being based very largely on cooperation and the voluntary adherence of sovereign states, are very fragile arrangements.

And the trading rules are among the most fragile. They are found at the intersection of relations between states and relations between powerful domestic interests and each national government. It is by way of trade that international relations impinge most directly upon the welfare of individuals and groups within the national economy. It is in this area, therefore, that it is extremely important to seek international disarmament. I am fearful that the resurrection of trade restrictions for balance-of-payments purposes will lead to an accelerated unraveling of the existing system, because we do not have sanctions adequate to protect the system. Measured retaliation, itself destructive of trade, is the only sanction today. Furthermore, it is extremely difficult to reverse this process once it is under way. Thus, while I fully understand why the Administration may want the right to raise tariffs on a nondiscriminatory and uniform basis, as a balance-of-payments weapon, I am uneasy about the implications and terribly uneasy about the rhetoric.

I don't like to play Cassandra. For the first time, however, I am a bit concerned that what began as a move toward greater flexibility in exchange rates at the Smithsonian in late 1971 may be turning into oligopolistic competition among governments seeking trading advantage. The entire system is in a precarious state, and I should hate to see our government take the lead in exposing it to new risks.

These are far from being operational recommendations for the future of the monetary system. I express them as I do only because I am extremely worried.

ROY BLOUGH: I think I agree with almost everything that Isaiah Frank and Peter Kenen have said. In this connection, I think it should be pointed out that devaluation can be regarded as a form of protection. And the reason that devaluation is politically acceptable is that nobody notices that it is a system of protectionism. That may be partly because, like monetary policy within a country, devaluation doesn't seem to discriminate against anybody. It is probably better than other forms of protection in avoiding wrong shifts in the use of resources.

I certainly would agree with Isaiah that more should be done within the U. S. government toward the harmonization of monetary and trade policies. Perhaps this Administration will succeed where others have failed. Of course, one of the problems is that monetary experts rarely are trade experts, and trade experts are rarely monetary experts; each group likes to go off and do its own negotiating. It is only an accident if the resulting efforts are consistent.

I also agree with Isaiah that we are going to have to deal with the problem of market disruption. I think the uniform import surcharge is so much superior to existing balance-of-payments measures authorized by the General Agreement on Tariffs and Trade that it is well worth trying. At the same time, I certainly agree with Peter Kenen that there is always the danger of reversing progress painfully achieved in the liberalization of international trade. The Tariff Act of 1930 left Congress in a completely traumatized condition which I think, unfortunately, it has gotten over. Forty years have disposed of most of the people who were traumatized in 1930, and I am afraid that we may have more difficulty making progress in trade policy in the future than in the past for the simple reason that so many people have died off.

RANDALL HINSHAW: I agree with almost all that Isaiah said, with all that Peter said, and with most of what Roy Blough said, but I am disturbed by the suggestion that import taxes are in some sense an equivalent of devaluation and an acceptable substitute for realistic exchange rates. As Gottfried Haberler pointed out many years ago, a devaluation is really a combination of two things: a uniform tax on imports and other international payments and a subsidy on exports and other international receipts. If a country suffering from inflation deals with its payments deficit by means of import taxes alone, then, as it gets into a steadily worsening payments position, it may eventually end up with no trade at all—no exports and no imports. This might not be serious for the United States—although I think it would be very serious—but it would be intolerable for most countries. If we are going to start talking about import taxes as a solution for payments problems, then I think we should also start talking about export subsidies—though I am certainly not recommending this approach.

BLOUGH: May I say that I agree completely with Randall Hinshaw and that every time I have written or spoken on this matter, I have included export subsidies for the reason he mentioned.

GOTTFRIED HABERLER: Do you really mean that devaluation is a protectionist device?

BLOUGH: Sure, you bet.

HABERLER: But if you say that, you could also say that free trade is protectionist, because a free-trade country may have to devalue if it inflates too much. It surely makes no sense to say that a free-trade country which has to devalue thereby becomes a protectionist country. Devaluation and protection have nothing to do with each other except in the sense that they may both help the balance of payments. It does not seem to me at all helpful to say that devaluation corrects the balance of payments by protectionist means.

If I may say a little more, I fully agree with Peter Kenen. I think it is really distressing and discouraging to listen to an economist substituting protection and quotas for devaluation. If economists agree on anything, then it is that free trade, or freer trade, is a good thing—yet here we go in exactly the opposite direction. I would agree with Isaiah Frank and Roy Blough that import surcharges are better than import quotas, but if we supplement import surcharges with export subsidies, as Professor Blough suggests, then the approach is equivalent to devaluation.

Of course, some will say that devaluation doesn't help. But if devaluation doesn't help, it can be shown that import restrictions, especially if they are of the general kind, won't help either—and that makes absolutely no sense. If an import surcharge helps, then a surcharge plus export subsidies—the equivalent of devaluation—will help even more. Thus it makes no sense whatever to substitute import restrictions for devaluation.

Chairman THORP: Isaiah has the floor.

FRANK: Just to clarify a couple of points. At first, I thought Gottfried was accusing me of advocating quotas for balance-of-payments reasons, but then I realized that I was not his target. But I want to make it perfectly clear that the import-surcharge proposal is not a substitute for exchange-rate changes. Everyone recognizes that. But in the absence of ability to accomplish in short order a more effective and more flexible exchange-rate system, a holding operation may be needed.

Turning to this question of symmetry, the economic arguments are impeccable for action both on the import and on the export side. But again we have to look at other considerations. Countries are much more willing to have you protect your own market than to have you subvene the penetration of their markets, and they can offset—and would have a legal right to offset—any export subsidies with countervailing duties. And they would probably do it. The reason for not combining import taxes with export subsidies is not an economic reason—on economic grounds, I completely agree with Randall Hinshaw's arguments in terms of resource allocation. The reason is that you could probably get away with an import tax but not with an export subsidy. In other words, the justification is strictly faute de mieux. But an import tax does distort. There is no question that action on the one side distorts resource allocation much more than symmetrical action on both sides.

HENRY C. WALLICH: I think we face a very long-run problem as well as the immediate strategic problem in our efforts to tie together trade negotiations and international monetary reform. Isaiah Frank has referred to the poor elasticities that we face, and has raised the question whether, under such conditions, we can hope to make our way in the world on the basis of a continuing freer-trade policy.

This is certainly not a new proposition. It is given some additional urgency by what we have learned about elasticities through recent events—notably, the continued deterioration in the U. S. balance of payments despite dollar devaluation. It is also given additional urgency by the energy problem. If it is true that the United States is going to need $1 billion in added imports each year for that purpose alone, it is going to be very difficult to make ends meet on a free-trade basis. At least we ought to confront that problem.

It may be that we have reached the point where we ought to look toward a lower level of trade, concentrating on things we badly need and trying to maintain good terms of trade for those products rather than aiming at the largest possible trade under less favorable terms. I would never have said this a few years ago; I find myself pushed in that direction by recent events. In fact, I would never have said a few years ago that the United States needed to worry about imports at all. I would have said that we should buy whatever we need from abroad and let the world decide what kind of an international trade system it wants. What we see now is that the United States is becoming an increasingly open economy, with a rising propensity to import. U. S. exports have not improved relative to GNP, and at some point it seems to me that a basic review of that situation is required. I have no firm opinion on these matters, and I would be greatly relieved if somebody could convince me that the old principles are still the right ones. But in the meantime, I think we need to stop, look, and listen.

ARTHUR B. LAFFER: Let me just make a brief comment on the proposition that devaluation is equivalent to an import tax plus an export subsidy. From a purely practical standpoint, I don't think they are equivalent. In most cases, when an import surcharge is levied, it does not apply to all goods and services; for example, many commodities were exempted from the import surcharge levied by the United States in 1971. Another difference is that an import tax provides revenue to the treasury, and thus reduces the budget deficit as well as the payments deficit.

HINSHAW: I think Art would agree that if the import tax is combined with an equivalent export subsidy, and both are applied across the board, the net effect on the budget is neutral when imports equal exports, is favorable when imports exceed exports, and is unfavorable when exports exceed imports.

KENEN: Mr. Chairman, I must dissent from what I take to be the spirit of Henry Wallich's comment and the spirit of something which Isaiah said earlier. Implicit in both of their statements was the assertion or suggestion that the marriage—the shotgun wedding—of trade and monetary negotiations favored by the United States is a desirable or optimal strategy from an economic or political point of view. Related to the misgivings I expressed earlier is my fear that the commitment to begin trade negotiations will be a millstone around our necks and the necks of our partners. At this stage, no one is ready for trade negotiations. No country can equip itself with adequate bargaining power—with adequate executive flexibility—without offering very expensive hostage to fortune.

The U. S. Administration may have to pay a high political price to obtain from Congress an adequate mandate to negotiate. At this juncture, moreover, our principal trading partners, the Europeans and the Japanese, are not at all interested in negotiating with us. Surely the revaluation of the yen will not make the Japanese government more receptive to extensive import liberalization—liberalization, by the way, which might have been much more valuable to the United States than the appreciation of the yen, since many Japanese import restrictions are quantitative and, therefore, completely frustrate the operation of the price and exchange-rate mechanism.

I have a certain pessimism about the prospect for negotiations and a profound fear of the consequences of failure. With particular reference to what Henry Wallich said, I find it paradoxical that, at a time when the United States is becoming increasingly aware of its own import dependence, illustrated dramatically by energy, it is becoming more bellicose and more unilateralist than it has been for a long time. At a time when there is an urgent need for stable trading rules, I sense a greater willingness to take risks with those rules and to threaten abrupt unilateral change in them. Now, bearing in mind that we are trying at the same time to rebuild the international monetary system, can we afford to jeopardize confidence in the trading rules? Perhaps I am being too pessimistic, but I doubt that next fall's deadline for new trade negotiations will prove to be happy for any of the parties concerned.

Sir ROY HARROD: Just a few words. I was delighted with the remark by Isaiah Frank that full employment must have priority over free trade as a target. That is a matter of the utmost importance, and I hope that there is now general agreement on this proposition.

As I said earlier, devaluation may make the balance of payments worse. Perhaps the British devaluation of 1967 helped matters a bit, but it took a long time—about two years—and the help did not come on the import side at all, because imports zoomed up at a greater rate than before. But there was some benefit on the export side. In the German case, currency appreciation doesn't seem to have reduced the payments surplus. So I don't think we should take it for granted that changes in exchange rates automatically promote adjustment.

This brings me to the subject of import controls. As I have said before, I think this may be almost a necessary weapon. Of course there are political consequences in relations with other countries. What this means to me is that the matter should be handled by an international body which says that, if other methods are not likely to be effective in a given situation, then it is proper for a country in deficit to use import restrictions. At the same time, the international body should be able to say to a country in surplus that it has an obligation to reduce its import barriers. These two aspects should be complementary.

WILSON E. SCHMIDT: In Isaiah's very perceptive review of the current situation, there is perhaps one element that he did not mention—namely, that the protectionists in the United

States are clearly using the current international monetary difficulties, which may well continue, as an excuse to justify such things as the Burke-Hartke bill. This suggests to me that, in the absence of a substantial monetary reform which will ease the international monetary situation, the possible answer to the protectionists is to divert their attention from the value of imports and to ask them to concentrate instead on the price of imports coming into the United States. I say this because, as Dick Cooper mentioned yesterday, there appears to have been a significant worsening of U. S. terms of trade, and that fact presumably raises the profit margins on much domestic production very substantially. If we can persuade the protectionists to think more about the reduction of import competition resulting from recent realignments in exchange rates, perhaps this will divert their attention from the international monetary system.

SEYMOUR E. HARRIS: I generally approve of Professor Frank's statement, which I thought was very good. I think he did not mention exchange control. He talked about exchange adjustments and related matters but, after all, exchange control is the most comprehensive type of control, and it should certainly be considered on its own merits.

FRANK: Exchange control in what sense?

HARRIS: I mean simply as a method of controlling the market for imports or anything else for which people want foreign exchange.

FRANK: Well, in that sense, it seems to me that exchange controls and quantitative import restrictions are almost proxies for each other.

HARRIS: No, exchange control is a much broader category.

FRANK: You mean comprehensive exchange controls applying to the capital side as well as to the current account. I haven't discussed the capital side at all.

Chairman THORP: This remark clearly brings us to the key issue of how international monetary reform can best deal with the problem of capital movements—particularly of the kind which has led to recent crises—and I propose that we now turn to that subject.

VIII. KEY ISSUES: THE PROBLEM OF CAPITAL MOVEMENTS

*Richard N. Cooper and
Members of the Conference*

The monetary crises of the late 1960s and early 1970s were characterized by—and, in an immediate sense, were caused by—massive international capital movements which in turn were motivated by anticipated changes in exchange rates. While such capital movements are often referred to as "speculative," it would be more accurate in many cases to describe them as prudential. Multinational corporations, for example, must constantly decide what is the best currency distribution in which to maintain their liquid assets—assets which initially are acquired as earnings in what is often a wide variety of currencies. Here the problem is not simply to maximize potential gains but to avoid catastrophic losses. In any case, the resulting corporate decisions contributed heavily to the disruptive "billion-dollar days" referred to by Frank Southard at the opening session, and such capital movements constitute one of the most perplexing problems in international monetary reform. More specifically, the problem facing reformers is how to deal with short-term capital movements of this character without interfering with productive long-term foreign investment of the type urgently needed, in particular, by the developing countries. This problem was the last topic considered by the conference.

R. H.

Chairman THORP: From time to time, members of the conference have referred to the problem of massive short-term capital flows and, in varying degrees, have indicated that virtually no monetary machinery, as such, could take care of the billions of dollars per day that Frank Southard has talked about. I suggest that we now tackle this problem—not limiting ourselves merely to short-term capital movements, but exploring all aspects of international capital flows as they relate to international monetary reform. To start the dialogue, I am calling on Richard Cooper.

RICHARD N. COOPER: Let me begin with a world view of short-term capital movements. There is, I think, a general presumption among economists in favor of free markets, including capital markets, on general allocative grounds. I would like to express some reservations—three in particular—as far as short-term capital movements are concerned. By short-term capital movements, I mean movements of funds from short-term money-market instruments in one currency or one country to another currency or country.

The first reason why the presumption in favor of unrestricted capital movements cannot be applied uncritically is that, under a regime of fixed exchange rates, short-term capital moves in response to divergences in national monetary policy. From a long-run allocative point of view, divergences in national monetary policy are transitory events. These policies are specifically designed to induce or restrain spending within a given domestic economy, and the central bank deliberately makes monetary conditions easier or tighter in order to eliminate a short-term disequilibrium in aggregate demand. Under these conditions, it defeats the purpose of monetary policy, in a regime of fixed exchange rates, to allow unrestrained movements of short-term capital. A country that attempts to tighten up on monetary conditions in order to restrain a domestic boom finds itself instead simply attracting large amounts of funds from abroad. This type of capital movement, motivated by cyclical divergences in interest rates, serves no social purpose; indeed, it tends to defeat the social purpose of monetary policy.

Secondly, capital movements that are in anticipation, rightly or wrongly, of changes in exchange rates serve no social purpose other than to signal the monetary authorities that exchange rates need to be changed. Unfortunately, that may be a necessary purpose in today's world, although im-

provements in the adjustment process presumably would
eliminate that purpose also. Otherwise, such movements
merely result in arbitrary transfers of purchasing power
from one country to another.

Thirdly, in the real world, we know that capital movements
respond to a considerable extent to fiscal incentives. It is no
secret that a large part of the attractiveness of the Eurodollar
market arises from the fact that, as a practical matter, interest earned there goes tax-free, whereas interest earned
in national money markets is taxable. Once again—assuming
that taxes serve legitimate social purposes—free capital
movements, under conditions of divergent tax arrangements,
may lead to misallocation.

For all of these reasons, and especially for the first, it
seems to me that, under a regime of fixed exchange rates,
one could make a very strong argument for maintaining controls on short-term capital movements. I should say at once
that the conditions I have identified apply not only to short-term capital flows but indeed to many kinds of international
transactions. The reason for focusing on short-term capital
movements is that the frictions inhibiting the movement of
short-term capital are very much less than they are for other
types of transactions and, therefore, the misallocation that
can arise from having unrestrained short-term movements is
correspondingly greater.

Having said all of that, I must now introduce a somewhat
despairing note—namely, that in today's world it is very hard
to make controls on capital movements stick. The public is
constantly becoming more imaginative in finding its way
around any given set of controls. Short-term capital can move
in the guise of practically any form of international transaction.
Therefore, while I think an allocative case can be made for
controls on short-term capital flows, I am far from optimistic
about the prospects for effective control. Saying that is not
the same as saying one should give up controls altogether. One
can view them as introducing one more friction which slows
down the responsiveness of the system—and this may be desirable. But it would be a mistake to expect to get 100 percent
effective controls; one can hope only to impede these movements, without actually eliminating them.

In the longer run, I believe that the tendency for the world
economy to become more and more integrated is so strong
that if we allow ourselves to look ahead twenty or thirty years,

we will find that, under a regime of fixed or even adjustable exchange rates, we cannot have independent national monetary policy. It will just be impossible to sustain. We may also find that fiscal evasion becomes so great that we cannot even have divergent tax rates—or more than modestly divergent tax rates—on interest earnings.

Attaining the political capacity to recognize and deal with these developments is the major agenda item for the world economy in the next couple of decades, and it is partly for this reason that I find myself more attracted to exchange-rate flexibility than I might otherwise be. Quite apart from considerations of balance-of-payments adjustment, which is the usual reason for emphasizing flexibility, exchange-rate flexibility introduces a barrier of uncertainty—a modest one, to be sure—between national economies. As long as the unit of responsibility and the unit of decision-making in economic policy is the national government—even though that is inconsistent with basic long-run tendencies in the world economy—one can view some degree of rate flexibility as a kind of holding operation while our political capacity catches up over time with the underlying integrative tendencies in the world economy.

Chairman THORP: A number of members have asked for the floor. The first is Sir Roy.

Sir ROY HARROD: There is only one point I would like to make about capital movements—a comment on the notion that investment abroad has an adverse effect on the balance of payments. Well, that is so only if one looks at the matter from a purely static point of view. If one makes an investment abroad in 1973, in that year the investment will have been a minus item in the balance of payments. But in subsequent years, there is a plus item coming in. Investment abroad is made for the express purpose of earning interest or profit, and, over a long enough period of time, the interest and profit exceeds the amount of the original investment.

In a dynamic analysis, we don't just look at capital investment in a certain year. If we look at the outgoing stream of capital investment and the incoming stream of interest and profit, the whole thing is favorable to the investing country. By the same token, it will be unfavorable—from a payments standpoint—for the countries in which the capital is invested. I have a good deal of sympathy with some of the less developed countries, particularly India. The Indians are very good economists. Some people think that the Indians resist capital imports because they don't like being taken over—because, in other words, they don't like to move from British imperialism to American imperialism. But I don't think that this is their main objection; as very good economists, they know perfectly well that if they allow a lot of capital in, it will be bad for their balance of payments.

COOPER: With regard to Sir Roy's argument, I think it is a fundamental mistake to assess the merits of international capital movements on the basis of their balance-of-payments effects. Of course it is true that if an investment pays off, the amount that is taken out over the whole stream of time will exceed the amount that goes in—in balance-of-payments terms. But that is no argument against investment from the viewpoint of the debtor country.

HARROD: I agree entirely with what Professor Cooper says—that we don't want to judge the importance and value of capital investment simply by its balance-of-payments effect. That's only one item. Of course there are other more important considerations. But we must get the balance-of-payments effect straight.

ISAIAH FRANK: I wonder if I might comment on Sir Roy's argument. It seems to me that his analysis should be extended to an examination of the other indirect consequences of foreign investment. There is a presumption, at least, that to some extent the production resulting from the investment might be import-substituting or might be export-creating, in which case one would have to look at the trade effects of the investment. When one does that, I am not sure that one could leap to Sir Roy's conclusion. The effects are surely more complex than suggested by his remarks.

HARROD: If I may just comment. What the developing countries need is the know-how that comes from abroad. That they need. They can supply the capital themselves; there's no problem there—they can supply the capital, they can't supply the know-how. And, therefore, those who are interested in international operations of a do-good character, as I hope we are here, should want as little as possible movement of capital to these developing countries, with as much as possible movement of know-how. The developing countries can pay a good price for the know-how. Indians can pay high prices to American technologists who tell them how to do this and that. But what the Indians don't want is the imported capital, because that's a burden to them. They have to pay for the know-how, but that is over and done with when the expert goes home.

SVEN W. ARNDT: I would like to expand on one of the points to which Dick Cooper has alluded concerning the perspectives one might take of international capital movements.

One perspective is to observe the phenomenal growth in recent years of the multinational corporation, the multinational bank, and the large private operators in financial markets. In this trend toward international financial oligopoly, it would appear that governments in various countries are losing their policy-making sovereignty. A recent study by the U. S. Tariff Commission concludes that by the end of 1971 there were some $268 billion in private liquid funds outstanding. This figure exceeds by more than two times the world's aggregate reserve assets held by countries and international institutions.

In the light of these developments, I think that Dick Cooper is right in pointing out that a single country may encounter great difficulty in employing effective defensive devices against the threat of rapid and frequent shifts of funds; and it was interesting to note that Dick concluded by saying that, more than any other consideration, it is this threat which makes him an advocate of flexible exchange rates.

But what, if anything, do we learn from oligopoly theory? One thing we learn is that where there is an oligopolistic market structure, there is room for collusion. This raises another question: To what extent does the increasingly oligopolistic international financial structure strengthen whatever arguments have already been made in favor of collusion among governments, by which I mean international cooperation and coordination of policies?

There are two broad ways of looking at this matter. One would be to argue, as frequently has been argued, that governments ought to collude—that is to say, ought to coordinate their policies against private operators in the market, since the domain of operations for some of these private operators actually exceeds the policy domain of some countries, and may overlap a number of national policy domains.

The other possible way of looking at collusion would be to examine the extent to which governments might collude with, rather than against, certain private operators. I'm not saying that this would necessarily be good for the world, but there may be ways in which governments might effectively collude in a positive social manner with private operators. One way might be to break down the distinction between official reserves and private reserves—between official liquid capital and private liquid capital. One might think in terms of encouraging private holdings of an international reserve asset in order, among other things, to soak up large private holdings of other liquid assets.

JOHN EXTER: What I have to say this morning is particularly pertinent to the subject of capital flows. It is also an attempt, Mr. Chairman, to get the subject of debtor-creditor relationships and interest rates—relative interest rates—on the agenda. These matters are much more important than some of the things we have been discussing, such as exchange-rate policy. On the latter matter, I would simply say that we are now basically in a floating exchange-rate world and that the exchange-rate policy of every country has to be to prevent the rate from rising and, if possible, to get it down. Central banks will have to be prepared to acquire assets—either domestic assets or U. S. dollar assets—in almost any amount in order to achieve this purpose.

To show you how debtor-creditor relationships figure in my mind, let me use the example of Japan. I am going to say a startling thing. To my mind, the Japanese yen today is grossly overvalued in the foreign-exchange marketplaces, and the dollar is undervalued. Why? We have been through a period of about three years in which people throughout the world have borrowed dollars and bought yen. The Bank of Japan has had to buy those dollars, which for the most part have been invested in U. S. government securities. Robert Triffin's frightening table shows some of the results of these purchases and purchases by other central banks. They contribute enormously to the growth of the credit pyramid that I keep in my mind, but what I now want to show is how all this affects future capital flows. The people who have borrowed dollars have dollar liabilities in the billions and corresponding assets in Japanese yen, on which they now have very considerable paper profits. This means that the dollar today is, technically speaking, extremely short in terms of yen. It is a very vulnerable situation. There are many inflationary bubbles in the world, but, to my mind, the biggest bubble of all is the bubble of dollars that have been borrowed to buy yen, which in turn have been used to buy stocks in the Tokyo stock exchange. We all know that bubbles cannot go on growing forever.

Chairman THORP. John, you have only one more minute.

EXTER: Don't you like what I say?

Chairman THORP: Don't ask me that. I just wish to say that there is a debtor-creditor relationship here. You promised to take three minutes; you've taken four already.

EXTER: I'm sorry. Well, what will happen is that at some point people will realize that the yen is overvalued and that they must try to realize their paper profits. It is as though an American bank had, as its principal asset, loans to Penn Central. This is a comparable situation. When the tide turns, as it inevitably will, people are going to get out of yen as fast as they can. Of course, many of them won't be able to get out, because the Bank of Japan will not sell the dollars back; it would much prefer to have the yen float downward in this world of competitive exchange depreciation.

I hope to come to our next conference in 1975. I think there will be much more chance of my getting there if I put some of my meager assets in gold coins rather than in shares in the Tokyo stock exchange. Even if the privilege is extended to me, you can be sure that I will not put any of my money in SDRs. As a matter of fact, I feel like Milton Gilbert, who has said that he will believe in SDRs when his wife asks for a bracelet made of them!

FRITZ MACHLUP: Mr. Chairman, I have noticed a general downgrading—not by Exter, but by almost all others—of the importance of capital movements and a general support of governmental controls and restrictions on international capital flows. I would therefore like to use my few minutes in defense of international capital movements.

Let me immediately make the usual distinction between short-term, or temporary and reversible flows, and long-term flows. Unfortunately, I see no practical way of distinguishing between the two. The criteria used by statisticians make no economic sense, and any controls that try to discriminate among various forms of instruments are likely to be ineffective, because capital flows can take a variety of forms. Moreover, it is very difficult to restrict short-term flows without restricting long-term flows. Of course, I am talking primarily in defense of long-term capital flows. I believe that such flows have been of the greatest importance in economic development throughout the world. I find a strange contradiction here: those who say that international capital movements are not important and should be restricted are the very same people who cry out for more financial aid to the less developed countries. Why should capital be unimportant if it is privately owned but terribly important if it is supplied by a government? The economic function is surely the same in both cases.

The idea of splitting the foreign-exchange market into financial transactions and commercial transactions is, I submit, foolish and nonsensical; it is based on a misunderstanding of the economic function of international capital flows. The economic function of such capital movements is to give the recipient country the opportunity of acquiring productive resources or commodities from other countries. In other words, a translation of financial flows into commercial flows is the essence of the process. To split the exchange market into financial transactions and commercial transactions is to prevent this translation. The splitters of the market insist that all the dollars that come from financial transactions should be used only by people who want to make the reverse movement—that is, by people who move dollars out again in financial transactions.

This amounts to what I call an "abortion" of the capital movement. The inward movement is allowed to take place, but it has to be reversed; in effect, it has to be aborted. I really don't understand why so many of my learned friends are in favor of such a splitting of the foreign-exchange market. I suspect that they are trying to protect vested interests, trying to prevent particular industries from losses and from the necessity to adjust to changes in market conditions.

ARNDT: I don't know whether Fritz included me in that group of learned friends.

MACHLUP: No, no, no; not at all.

ARNDT: Let me just clarify one point. You were talking about long-term capital movements. But I think we must make a sharp distinction between long-term and short-term capital movements.

PETER B. KENEN: My colleague, Fritz Machlup, is far too polite to suggest that I am capable of nonsense or foolishness, and I will spare him that necessity by saying myself that I am experimenting, intellectually, with some foolishness or nonsense. I have come to evince at least a certain sympathy for the dual-rate device.

Let me say right away that I agree fully with Professor Machlup that long-term capital movements have an enormously important functions to play. I also agree fully that one cannot distinguish statistically or administratively between long-term and short-term capital movements. The relevant distinction has to do with motivation, whereas the statistical and administrative distinctions have to do with the kind of assets that are bought or sold. If I buy short-term instruments and renew them indefinitely, I am involved in a long-term capital transaction, but an administrator would classify it as a short-term transaction. If I buy long-term instruments and sell them tomorrow, what would look like a long-term capital movement to an administrator is clearly a short-term movement. It is thus impossible to draw an operational distinction between long-term and short-term capital movements, and if one has capital controls, they probably have to extend uniformly over all capital movements.

Thus there are two questions. First, is there a case for having any controls on capital movements? Second, if one is to have controls, what kinds will be least obstructive to long-term flows motivated by differences in the marginal product of capital?

There is, I believe, some justification for capital controls. The case is precisely the one which Professor Machlup put the other way around. The transfer process is too often aborted. It is aborted by the decisions of governments which are reluctant to allow the exchange-rate change or internal adjustment required to accomplish a transfer of real resources. A firm making an investment in a foreign country is not interested in transferring real resources. That may be the economic function of the capital movement; it is not the motive of the capital mover. The economic function is performed by the adjustment process, which must be triggered by automatic market forces or by deliberate governmental actions. If governments choose to block the adjustment process, for good or bad reasons of their own, we face serious international monetary problems, and it may be necessary to curb the capital movements which generate those problems.

Let me say in passing to Sven Arndt that the issue here is not the size of the pool of internationally mobile funds in relation to the reserves of governments. The important comparison is between the monetary base in any medium-sized country and the amount of foreign money that can come in or move out to inflate or deflate the monetary base, wreaking havoc with the monetary policy of the country concerned. A country does not need reserves to stabilize its exchange rate in the face of a capital inflow. A central bank can always print its own money. What it does in the process, however, is to inflate the reserves of its banking system. Whether we like it or not, moreover, governments will seek to preserve national autonomy, including autonomy in the conduct of monetary policy.

Having said these things, what then is to be said for one type of capital control over another? It seems to me that the second-best alternative to a unitary fluctuating exchange rate of the kind which Dick Cooper has suggested would be a dual-rate system, in which a fluctuating rate applies specifically to capital movements. This approach is superior to direct controls, because it does not discriminate administratively and arbitrarily between one form of capital movement and another, and because it impedes capital flows by creating uncertainty concerning the exchange rate at which capital can be repatriated. This element of uncertainty may bear most harshly upon the short-term capital flows that have the least to contribute to efficient international resource allocation, the objective which Professor Machlup so correctly emphasized.

I am not enthusiastic about this approach. I start with the premise, however, that governments are going to seek autonomy in monetary policy for some time to come, no matter how we may try to educate them in the use of fiscal policy; and I doubt that governments are prepared to accept flexible exchange rates for trade transactions over the long term. I am therefore inclined to accept as the least of evils a splitting of capital and trade transactions by means of a dual exchange rate as an alternative to more severe quantitative controls on capital movements or, worse yet, on trade.

JAGDISH BHAGWATI: Fritz Machlup is so good at pointing out nonsense in other people that perhaps I should pay him back, with his permission, on a very minor point in this debate. Anybody who thinks that foreign aid is good is not necessarily obliged to think that long-term foreign investment is good, because aid is a different kind of dollar if it is genuine aid. Aid in the form of a grant does not have to be paid back. It is therefore perfectly possible, without committing an atrocity of logical inconsistency, for a person to hold the views on foreign aid and on capital controls which Professor Machlup finds so incompatible.

It seems to me that we all too frequently take it for granted that a flow of long-term capital is necessarily desirable from a world-efficiency point of view. This proposition is generally regarded as following symmetrically from the position—which I share—in favor of as much free trade as possible. But I am not sure that it applies in all cases. At the time of the Smithsonian agreement, I understand that Mr. Connally was putting pressure on Japan to open up the Japanese market to investment from abroad. I never really understood why, unless the idea was for major firms here to invest in Japan in order to get some return from Japanese competition rather than to compete here by producing similar products. Now if my suspicion is correct, then we are talking about a competition-reducing kind of investment, and I am not sure that this is a good idea. My own view, if I may spell it out, is that capital flows don't really belong to the same kind of field as trade flows. The same prescriptions don't necessarily apply, so I am not particularly disturbed by dual exchange rates or other types of control on international capital movements.

JOHN PARKE YOUNG: I agree very much with what Professor Machlup has said about the importance of international capital flows, particularly long-term investment. Our main problem in this field arises from short-term capital movements, which we all know can be very disturbing. Most of these movements are due to currency uncertainties and speculation induced by expected changes in exchange rates. This is perhaps the main reason why we need a numeraire for private transactions. I will not repeat the proposal I outlined earlier, but I think it would certainly assist in coping with the problems we have just been discussing.

IX. CONCLUDING REFLECTIONS

Lord Robbins

As at the earlier conferences in the Bologna-Claremont series, the Moderator was assigned the task, as the final item on the agenda, of summarizing the conference dialogue and, in particular, of identifying the areas of agreement and disagreement.

R. H.

Lord ROBBINS: Whatever our disagreements, I think we should all agree that this conference has been a very stimulating experience. I think it would be in order for me, in a very humble capacity indeed, to express my admiration for the high quality of the contributions which have been made in the course of our deliberations. I don't know what the rest of you think, but I certainly have learned a great deal.

While we have not achieved unanimity even as regards broad measures of policy, I do think that there has been a surprising absence of dissent around the table regarding ends as distinct from means. Gottfried Haberler reminded us that the world had jogged on at a smart pace despite all the anxious preoccupations of recent years. But I don't think that Gottfried himself—and I can't believe that anyone else—would wish to deny that the situation we have been living through has been implicit with grave danger. In a way, we've had an extraordinary run of good luck, aided and abetted by the informal conspiracy of men of goodwill throughout the free world, in

145

assuring that these financial convulsions have not led to a state of economic warfare such as we witnessed in the 1930s. I think it's important to recognize that, although we've had good luck so far, it would be wishful thinking to assume that this will last in the absence of continual vigilance.

Now it's my dreadful job this morning to try to get the highlights into perspective, and that job has not been made any easier by our gigantic banquet last night, which involved my rising at a very early hour this morning in order to review the voluminous bundle of notes which I felt it my duty to take as the conference proceeded. I must apologize to you, having regard to the time at my disposal, if I do not mention all the names of those who participated. I would like to emphasize that where I do mention names, it is not to praise some more than others or to disagree with some more than others, but simply to make more vivid the recapitulation of different points of controversy.

I suppose the first matter to mention is the debt which we owe to those who have provided us with hitherto unrevealed information in the course of our deliberations. It would be a great pity, I think, if the record were to bear no evidence of our great indebtedness to Frank Southard and to Robert Solomon for speaking to us so frankly on matters on which an earlier generation of public servants, national and international, would have been more taciturn and secretive. I think we owe a great debt to Frank Southard for his illuminating summary of the financial history of the world in recent years and for his explanations concerning the way in which the Fund operates in regard to SDRs; and we owe an almost equal debt to Bob Solomon for the partial lifting of the veil on what goes on in the deliberations of the Committee of Twenty, of which he is such a distinguished member. I should like also, while I'm talking about the provision of information, to thank Robert Triffin for his statistical table and to say how much over the years we all owe to his accurate diagnosis of the situation boiling up in the world and to the stimulating hints that he has thrown out at successive Bologna-Claremont conferences as to the possibilities of amelioration.

Now as to the detail. As I see things, we can divide our appraisal under four headings. We discussed exchange-rate changes and adjustments. We discussed—and this is the most ambiguous of the titles—the question of the standard. We discussed the relationship between trade policy and international monetary reform. Finally, we gave some attention to capital movement. And that, at any rate, is the order in which I shall try to couch my recapitulation.

    To begin with exchange-rate changes, I suppose it was natural that our talk should be dominated by the events of the last few weeks, including the second devaluation of the dollar. But if one looks at matters from a great height, it is clear that in all the incidental gossip about these events, there were, dominating the conversation, two abstract questions. First of all, do changes in exchange rates work? And secondly, if they do work, what rules, if any, should prevail regarding their regulation and mode of operation?
    As regards the first of these questions—whether changes of rates work—discussion clearly was dominated by the challenge which was thrown down by Bob Mundell at quite an early stage concerning the future development of the U. S. balance of payments, having regard to the recent devaluation. Bob's argument, if I understand him correctly, was that the assumption prevalent in the thought of the 1930s—that devaluations could correct balance-of-payments deficits—no longer holds. The institutional framework is different, and the assumptions necessary to make regarding the behavior of governments are certainly different. Bob supported his point of view by citing a certain amount of alleged empirical evidence. He supported it further by the analytical argument that money illusion has vanished from the earth and that, although it would be wrong to say that exchange-rate changes have no effect, they chiefly affect internal price developments rather than the balance of payments.
    This point of view received a certain amount of support around the table. Frank Southard himself expressed some perplexity of mind concerning the outcome of the dollar devaluation, although at a later stage in the argument he intervened to emphasize that his pessimism in that respect, even if it were justified, would not bear generalization. There was a certain amount of support for this position from Roy Harrod, who insisted then and at later stages that everything depends upon elasticities and that there is no watertight overall presumption that devaluations always work the right way.
    But I think it would be fair to say that these points of view were challenged from many quarters in the conference. As I've said already, Frank Southard himself intervened to warn

against any generalization of his pessimism. Fritz Machlup pointed out how misleading it may be to argue <u>post hoc ergo propter hoc</u> from the history of time series after devaluations. He argued with considerable force that a devaluation might be successful if it merely arrested a certain deterioration. And Gottfried Haberler produced what I thought was a very strong argument by citing the negative example of the Latin American countries which have been compelled in a state of more or less nonstop inflation to make periodic devaluations of their currencies. In that connection, Gottfried argued, would it really be contended that their position would be better if these devaluations had not taken place? Fritz Machlup intervened again to recall an earlier phase of discussions of this sort— the atmosphere of the period immediately after the war when some econometricians, who should have known better, presented us with the most alarming estimates of unfavorable elasticities, which nothing that has happened since has done anything to support.

Peter Kenen attempted, I thought not without some force, a certain reductio ad absurdum, I won't say of Bob's position (it would be frightfully difficult to reduce Bob to an absurdity in any context whatever), but a reductio ad absurdum of what some simpliste interpretation of Bob's position might suggest— namely, that if it were true, it would lead to inverse policies. Countries with an adverse balance of payments would appreciate their rates of exchange and surplus countries would depreciate—quite a strong debating argument, whatever the ultimate analytical penumbra thereof.

I personally must express a certain amount of sympathy with Bob's critics. Bob made some allusion to the purchasing-power-parity theory of the foreign exchanges. Well, I was brought up on that. I gradually came to realize that it was far too simple an account even of the old classical theory, let alone of the more modern apparatus that we can bring to bear. But reverting to that point of view for a moment, let us suppose that there are two communities, A and B, which have been in equilibrium as regards exchange rates and relative price levels. Now suppose that in community A there takes place a halving of the value of money by an inflationary movement, everything else remaining constant. Is it really to be denied that acute disequilibrium would follow in the balance of payments—a disequilibrium which could be put right by an appropriate devaluation? I don't say that this presumption would necessarily hold in regard to more complex situations. Certainly, it would not hold if there were additional complications arising from the fact that the real forces of supply and demand were changing in perverse directions at the same time.

But one always has to take Bob seriously; at any rate, that has been my motto in life ever since I had the privilege of getting to know him. And I've spent the last two days wondering what really it is that is worrying him—why he is led to this slogan about the erosion of money illusion—and I think the fact is that Bob is asking us to operate, and is perhaps operating in his own mind, with a model in which the internal conduct of monetary policy is completely elastic—a Tookean model, so to speak, in which money is completely responsive to the alleged needs of trade.

Now I find it difficult to think of any competent economist who would deny that, in circumstances of that sort, a devaluation would probably prove to be nugatory. Indeed, I seem to remember, Bob—and it's a long time since I've refreshed my memory—a classic chapter or series of chapters in James Meade's monumental work, in which he works out exactly the relationship between a given change in the exchange rate and an appropriate adjustment of monetary policy which would make that change effective. Now I suspect that those of us who don't go all the way with Bob, while I hope that we don't cherish infantile delusions about the probable rationality of government, do certainly postulate that in order that devaluations, when we recommend them, should be effective, the government should be told to pursue an appropriate internal policy. And I would suggest that recent British experience goes some way to prove that.

Thus, after the devaluation of 1967, there was not only the degree of perverse reaction which one would expect of a devaluation of that sort in the short period; the disequilibrium persisted for many months, and the reason I, at any rate, would give for that fact was that, until there had been a certain amount of peaceful persuasion by David Finch and officials of the International Monetary Fund, the then Chancellor of the Exchequer took neither fiscal nor monetary measures which were at all likely to make the devaluation effective. Once things had been tightened up in the appropriate way, it was quite extraordinary the rapidity with which we developed an unprecedented export surplus.

But so much for the effectiveness of changes in exchange rates. Our next question was that, assuming that rate changes work sometimes, how should they be operated? What should be the international rules of the game? And in that connection, I thought that Robert Solomon's classification of the possibilities which are presenting themselves to the Committee of Twenty was a very valuable contribution to one's thought on this subject. There seemed to emerge—possibly because of incautious and insufficiently qualified statements on my part— a certain difference of opinion about the degree of automatism that was desirable in this connection. At any rate, I detected around the table a considerable support for some degree of automatism.

On this matter, I would beg your indulgence for a little clarification of my own attitude. Introspectively, I certainly am conscious of a strong penchant for rules and for automatism where they can be rationally justified, and I would not object to a series of presumptions such as those implied by the first of Solomon's three alternative groups of policy. The idea that, when losses or gains of reserves have reached a certain point, this should be the occasion for consultation—or even the occasion for actions to be taken—I should not find at all antipathetic. My trouble is perhaps a certain negative reaction to the insistence which I have sometimes detected in talking to friends on this side of the Atlantic that it's the surplus countries which are always at fault and that one should therefore have no compunction whatever in roping them into a pretty rigid system of operation in this respect.

But surely it's not true that surplus countries are always at fault. Surely that has not been true in the postwar period. I really have very great sympathy for friends in Germany (who on the whole are very prone to agonizing reappraisals—at any rate, among professional economists) when they feel that they are being a little hardly done by in being held up to a politically difficult program simply because, owing to their superior prudence, learned through two bitter experiences of hyperinflation, they have inflated less than other people and, in consequence of that prudence, have reaped results in the shape of reserves growing at what, from the British point of view, seems to be a most enviable rate.

Now I would agree with the critics that reluctance to change may often be a sign of wrongheadedness. I would agree with Gottfried, for instance, that it probably was rather wrongheaded on the part of the German authorities not to decide to float at the time the massive transfers began. But as I have said, a surplus may be the result of other people's inflation. Currency appreciation is not always politically an entirely painless policy, and a surplus country may, on occasion, feel a certain reluctance to be pushed into doing something politically difficult just because other people have been much less prudent than the surplus country itself.

Well, so much for the first group of questions—the effects of exchange-rate changes and the rules governing them. Now we come to an area in which I must say that, at half-past six this morning, I found it much more difficult to get my ideas into any sort of logical order. And I don't think that this was altogether due to the hour or to my own natural befuddlement of mind. Nor, Mr. Chairman, was it in the least due to your conduct of the proceedings, which was masterly. What would have happened in the absence of such conduct, imagination boggles at.

Let us start from the beginning here. The background of our discussion, of course, was Frank Southard's extremely illuminating statement concerning the administration of the SDR account in the Fund, and from that there sprang discussions which related either to the question of where we ought to go eventually or to the question of how we ought to get there from here. And I do submit, in all humility and consciousness of my own amateurishness in handling these matters at this time of life, that the distinction between these two rather different questions was not always rigidly observed in the observations which came up from various parts of the table.

I think we all agree that the recent position of the dollar was unsatisfactory and that the asymmetry of the position of the dollar under the Bretton Woods statutes had turned out, contrary to any expectations of the founders, to be an embarrassment all around—an embarrassment to the rest of the world and certainly, in the last stages, an embarrassment to the unfloatable dollar. But while there was little apparent difference of opinion about that, the varieties of opinion on the question of where eventually to go were very great indeed.

At one hand, one had the courageous and inspiring exhortations of John Parke Young, recalling the proposal which he launched at the 1971 Bologna meeting—that the IMF should, so to speak, transform itself when practicable into an international central bank, with IMF money transferable and the bank itself open to receive deposits of all sorts. At the other end of the spectrum—well, not quite at the other end, because John Exter doesn't believe in any of this stuff and wishes that it could be abolished in favor of something nearer his heart's desire—was Frank Southard's very cautious indication of what, in his view, were the possibilities in the near future for extensions of the role of the SDR. He certainly was not negative in this respect. He revealed possibilities which, in his judgment, were practical and which, certainly from the point of view of people with moderate expectations like myself, seemed to open vistas of gradual evolution in a more rational direction.

But I would venture the general observation that much of the discussion at that stage and at that level—the discussion of where eventually we want to go—took a great deal for granted as regards the future political organization of the world. No one would be more pleased than I should be to think that the free world was so politically organized as to involve as a logical consequence the setting up of a central bank whose common money would eliminate most of the difficulties that we've been discussing in the last two days. But the free world is not so politically organized; and I fancy that if our discussions were taking place, not in the United States nor even, perhaps, in the United Kingdom, and if the membership of the conference were appropriately changed, there would be all sorts of political reservations popping up from time to time. Indeed, Mr. Schleiminger let one or two of them out of the bag in the course of his observations, leaving the impression to the impartial onlooker that progress is going to be rather more difficult than we've been apt to assume around this table.

Conspicuous as a development of the discussion at this level, I think, was Fritz Machlup's masterly elucidation of the meaning in this context of the concept of numeraire. I always feel a cad when I disagree with Fritz—and I do disagree with him a little bit about international monetary policy—but I was happy to note that, although his spiritual eye was focused on moon dust, he tried to bring the conference down to earth by suggesting that members of the conference ought possibly to limit their ambition to using the SDR as a numeraire.

The question is: Can SDRs in any near future perform the functions of world money, or free-world money, as would be so agreeable to many of us? Richard Cooper doubted that it

would be practicable in the near future, but he submitted that
SDRs as at present conceived did not go far enough, and while
I don't know that he went quite so far as John Parke Young, he
did urge—with that beautiful lucidity and force which make
his exposition so enviable—the eventual need for transformation
of the IMF into a lender of last resort.

But all of this left the second question in the air—where to
go now. And Gottfried Haberler introduced a note of sober
realism into the discussion by insisting that, after all, despite
all the vicissitudes of the last few years, the world is still
effectively on a dollar standard. He wasn't content with that
state of affairs; he merely wanted us to see the world with
clear eyes, and he went on at once to suggest ways in which
this ambiguous situation could be made perhaps more tolerable to sensitive souls—central bankers and others—by providing a purchasing-power guarantee to official dollar holdings.
Richard Cooper asked: Why not extend the Haberler proposal
to other dollar holdings? Others who took part in the discussion at this stage were concerned with the convertibility of the
dollar, and the question arose in this connection: Is it conceivable that in the next few years the world will be prepared
to concede enough leeway to the U.S. economy for it to be
once more in surplus and to accumulate reserves adequate to
a position of dollar convertibility without grave danger?

This led to a discussion on various matters relating to the
role of gold. Bob Mundell drew our attention to the statement
by the Secretary of the Treasury at the moment of dollar devaluation, a statement which he tried to infuse with importance.
Mr. Solomon questioned whether Bob's reading of this statement would bear all the weight that Bob wanted to attach to it.
Possibly, Bob wanted to get a foot in the door about a state of
affairs which he found more congenial. Be that as it may.
Whatever interpretation is to be put on future U.S. policy in
regard to alteration of the price of gold and the way in which
that is related to SDRs, I think Frank Southard's sober statement of the possibilities of Congressional action really said
the last word about immediate probabilities.

There were hints thrown out that certain central banks
were contemplating inter-central-bank dealings in gold, not
at the official price, but rather at the market price. And the
question was raised—I'm not sure whether Bob actually articulated it in this way—well, what would happen if Europe as
a whole were to work on this basis? I am bound to say that I

do not regard this as being altogether out of the question. My own suspicion as regards the prospect of the next few years—and I hope the suspicion is wrong—is that governments are going to take a very, very long time to reach agreed conclusions on reform; whereas developments in Europe, although they will certainly not go—and I would not wish to see them go—rapidly toward a completely common money, will proceed, I should imagine, toward something like a European clearing union. By the time of our next conference, I would not be surprised to see something like arrangements for a combined European float vis-a-vis the dollar area, in which case all sorts of conjectures with regard to the future of the international monetary system might have to be revised. (Editor's Note: This prediction was largely fulfilled only a month after the conference. In March 1973, those Common Market countries whose currencies were not already floating agreed to a common float against the dollar. They were joined by Norway and Sweden.)

At this stage, there were various suggestions for ways of getting rid of gold. Richard Cooper, not so realistic as usual, thought that there might be a special issue of SDRs which would absorb the gold reserves of the great powers, the gold then being sold at the free-market price and the proceeds used to provide aid for underdeveloped countries. This was the occasion on which I felt least swayed by his persuasive eloquence. I simply hate to be the <u>Geist der stets verneint</u> in regard to the less developed countries. I repeat what I said at the beginning: I'm not in the least ashamed of being, jointly with others, one of the founders of the World Bank at Bretton Woods, and I certainly agree that it is the duty of Western countries to do what is within their power to ameliorate conditions in these parts of the world. But I must say that I simply do not see the political probability that any of the great central banks would be allowed to get away with the Cooper policy. It just isn't politically "on," and I think it is utterly unrealistic to assume that outside the United States—I wouldn't even say outside the United Kingdom—there would be much discussion of central banks parting with their gold reserves. Whatever they do with them while they have them, parting with them at less than the market price seems to me highly unlikely even if one ignores altogether what hasn't been mentioned at this conference—the defense considerations which affect the thinking of at least some treasuries in regard to gold.

My own feelings in this respect incline very much toward Frank Southard's cautious views. I hope that we get used to the SDRs. I certainly hope that they won't be issued in excess so as to give any further spur to international inflation. I hope that there will be a cautious extent to their use, which will certainly make international adjustment all around much easier. But I would hope that at this stage we don't frighten people too much by threats of demonetizing gold. John Exter, you know, is not the only man in the world who fears the possible breakup of the postwar monetary system. If this conference were being held in Europe, it wouldn't be at all difficult to go out into the street and come upon quite a number of people who still feel that the system is a bit phoney. I'm not approving of that; I just draw your attention to the fact that if you disregard that attitude—if you are thinking of roping in Europe, not to say Asia, into any revised international monetary arrangements— you may be in for severe disappointment. I can't believe that there will be a complete free-world money until there is much greater political unity than seems likely to occur in the near future.

There remains the great question of dollar overhang. Shall we see a great funding operation, or will Gottfried Haberler's splendid suggestion do? I don't know. I simply think that one should bear in mind all sorts of possibilities, and one of those possibilities may very well be that in the next few years there may emerge crises elsewhere in the world which will make a good many present expectations unreliable. Personally, I certainly would very much welcome the implementation of Gottfried's proposal but, not being a citizen of the United States, I don't know how politically acceptable it actually is.

Well, I need not go on much longer. The discussion under the heading of trade was, I think, an extremely interesting and illuminating one. I listened with great respect, although not with complete agreement, to Isaiah Frank's apologia for what he suggested might be the intention of the U. S. Administration in linking so intimately the prospective monetary and trade negotiations. But I must confess that in this connection my sympathies were all with Peter Kenen. I think the structure of demobilization of the obstacles to trade which grew up in the 1930s has been achieved with so much difficulty, and is so obviously politically vulnerable, that anything which allows protectionist influence to get a foot further in the door is to be regarded as dangerous.

We had a useful discussion at this stage on the parallelism between devaluation and protectionism, and I think it was a happy thing that Randall Hinshaw and Gottfried Haberler reminded us that the exact equivalent—or rather the nearer equivalent—of devaluation is not one-sided protectionism but the tariff-bounty idea which was floated in the early 1930s by Keynes: a duty on imports and a subsidy on exports. In this connection, there was some discussion of Roy Harrod's suggestion of quantitative regulation, and here—although I don't agree with him—I must leap to my dear friend's defense on this matter. I felt that the moral that was expressed or was implicit in some of the objections to his suggestion was misplaced, and that it is only right for your Moderator to emphasize that, whether or not you agree with Roy's suggestion, he is not asking you to step into an old-fashioned unilateral pair of trousers. His suggestion is that quantitative regulation should become one of the instruments of international supervision—that the imposition of quota controls in the presence of perverse elasticity in international trade should be regulated by world authority. Having said that, while I can see his argument in principle, I am bound to say that I think the practical difficulties of operating that particular structure would speedily prove to be such as to make Roy himself reconsider his position.

Finally, we come to the question of capital movements. As most of that discussion took place this morning, you must excuse me if I fail to give you a very lucid or coherent account of all the issues involved. I must say that I agreed root and branch with Fritz Machlup's emphasis on the beneficial effect of long-term capital investment. And I am sure that Fritz would accept at once the Bhagwati footnote to this, emphasizing that there is a difference—a recognizable difference—between aid and capital investment, but I think that leaves the general analytical bearing of Fritz's position unaltered.

If there is any doubt on this matter, I ask members of the conference to take a broad view of history and possible history. Contrast the evolution of Canada and the United States under the influence of capital investment from the other side of the Atlantic with the ardors and agonies inflicted—self-inflicted—in the USSR in the absence of capital investment of that sort from abroad. How different, how much more humane, would have been the evolution of economic conditions in Russia had the Revolution not taken place—had that great area been open to massive investment from the wealthier parts of the world. Hence I'm a Machlup man in this respect.

I'm a Machlup man also as regards his strictures on capital control. Of course I agree with Richard Cooper's acute remarks about the dubious value of certain short-term capital movements and their profoundly disturbing effects on the present structure of the international monetary system. Who could possibly deny that? But the problem of disentangling beneficial long-term investment from these perverse short-term movements seems to me to be administratively overwhelming, and I'm not really consoled by the report that Peter Kenen, with all his well-known ingenuity, is experimenting with the idea of a two-tier system. I can't help thinking that, when the laboratory experiments have been going on for some time, he may be forced to the conclusion, given his accustomed candor, that the game, after all, is not worth the candle. In any case, it is, I think, a worthwhile reflection at this stage to realize that these perverse movements are due either to political uncertainties which would not exist if there were more unity in the political organization of Western civilization or to exchange uncertainties which arise because we have found it necessary to introduce some degree of flexibility in the foreign-exchange market as a result of the national desire for financial autonomy.

Hence I conclude with extending the warmest welcome I can possibly evoke to Richard Cooper's concluding observation that he was in favor of a certain amount of flexibility in exchange rates in the hope that it would see the world through until we have achieved a more sensible political system in which we can have a common money—at any rate in the free world—and in which all the headaches which have given rise to this kind of conference would be nonexistent.

NAME INDEX

Arndt, Sven W., 138-39, 141, 142

Bernstein, Edward M., 4, 5, 6
Bhagwati, Jagdish, 66-67, 143-44, 156
Blough, Roy, 116, 126-28

Clower, Robert W., 65-66
Connally, John B., 144
Cooper, Richard N., 62-64, 98-100, 107, 115-16, 117-18, 132, 134-36, 137, 138, 143, 152-53, 154, 157

Douglass, Gordon K., 96-97, 98

Emminger, Otmar, 33
Fisher, Irving, 18
Frank, Isaiah, 45, 100-1, 121-25, 126, 128-29, 131, 132, 137, 155
Friedman, Milton, 10, 24, 81

Gilbert, Milton, 140
Glendinning, C. Dillon, 106

Haberler, Gottfried, 55-57, 58, 103-7, 112 116-17, 127-28, 145, 148, 150, 153, 155, 156
Harris, Seymour E., 66, 132
Harrod, Sir Roy, 50-51, 59, 66, 80, 88, 121 122, 131, 136-38, 156
Hawtrey, Sir Ralph, 47
Heilperin, Michael A., 80
Hinshaw, Randall, 1-10, 13, 81, 94, 95, 127, 130, 156

Jamison, Conrad C., 47

Kenen, Peter B., 53-54, 55, 90-93, 96, 97-98, 100, 106-7, 125-26, 127, 130-31, 141-43, 148, 155, 157

Keynes, Lord, 2, 57, 66, 81, 156
Kissinger, Henry A., 21
Laffer, Arthur B., 56, 60-61, 130
Law, John, 82
Lerner, A. P., 52

Machlup, Fritz, 51-53, 57, 61, 89, 107-8, 109-10, 111, 113, 114-15, 140-41, 142, 143, 144, 148, 152, 156, 157
Meade, J. E., 5-6, 149
Morse, Jeremy, 97
Mundell, Robert A., 43-50, 52, 53, 54, 55, 57, 58, 59, 61, 62, 63, 64, 66-67, 81, 89-90, 92, 108-9, 110, 111, 112, 113, 115, 118-19, 147-49, 153

Nixon, President Richard M., 16, 21, 81

Oliver, Robert W., 84-86

Robbins, Lord, 1, 8, 12, 13-27, 38, 45, 63-64, 81, 84, 85, 103, 106, 107, 145-57
Rueff, Jacques, 4, 5, 6, 80

Salant, Walter S., 49-50, 67-69, 88-89
Schleiminger, Guenther, 8, 29, 33, 39-41, 49, 63-64, 94-95, 96, 113, 115, 152
Schmidt, Wilson E., 97, 131-32
Scitovsky, Tibor, 59-60, 93-94, 95, 98
Shultz, George P., 13, 114, 117
Silk, Leonard S., 48-49, 65, 110, 114, 115
Smith, Adam, 116-17
Solomon, Robert, 8, 29, 34-39, 71, 78, 88, 90, 92, 96, 100, 110, 111-12, 114, 146, 150, 153
Southard, Frank A., Jr., 8, 29, 30-34, 35, 46, 61-62, 76-80, 90, 93, 94, 98, 109, 112-13, 118, 119, 133, 146, 147, 151, 152, 153, 155

159

NAME INDEX

Thorp, Willard L., 8, 9-13, 14, 29, 34, 39, 43, 45, 47, 48, 49, 50, 51, 54, 55, 57, 59, 60, 61, 62, 64, 67-68, 71-72, 75, 76, 80, 86, 88, 89, 90, 94, 97, 100, 103, 105, 107, 109, 110, 111, 113, 115, 119, 121, 128, 132, 134, 136

Triffin, Robert, 3, 4-5, 6, 72, 85, 86-88, 89, 90, 94, 112, 146

Volcker, Paul A., 66, 71

Wallich, Henry C., 57-59, 90, 95-96, 99, 117-18, 129-30

Walras, Leon, 107

Young, John Parke, 47, 72-76, 80, 85, 144, 151-52, 153

SUBJECT INDEX

Adjustment, international: theme of 1969 Claremont conference, 6, 11; and exchange-rate policy, 6, 41; and gold standard, 92; Cooper proposal, 99
Appreciation, currency, 9, 23-24, 63
Arbitrage, intra-European, 94
Articles of Agreement of IMF, 79, 115, 119
Asian Bank, 79
"August events" of 1971, 30
Austria, 55
Automaticity as an issue, 36

Bank for International Settlements (BIS), 79
Bank of Canada, 7
Bank of France, 2
Bank of Japan, 139-40
Bernstein reserve-unit proposal, 5
"Billion-dollar days," 30, 33, 133
"Blue gold," 115
Brazil, 56
Bretton Woods system, 9, 38, 84, 85
Burke-Hartke bill, 132

Canada, 47-48, 49, 84, 156
Canadian dollar. See Dollar, Canadian
Capital movements as a problem, 90-91, 99-100, 133-44, 156-57
Committee of Ten, 34
Committee of Twenty, 8, 34-39, 56, 92, 93, 97, 146
Common agricultural policy of EEC, 124
Compensated Dollar proposal, 18
Convertibility: return to in Western Europe, 2; problems created by return to, 3; and monetary reform, 37-38, 41, 98-100; proposal for partial asset settlement of deficits, 95-96
Council of Economic Advisers, 35
Cruzeiro, 56

"Deficits without tears," 5, 7
Design of reform, 71-119
Devaluation: meaning of in U. S. 1973 case, 45-46; Laffer views on, 60-61; versus import restrictions, 51, 122, 127, 130, 131, 156
Developing-country problems, 101, 136-37, 141, 143-44, 154
Dollar, Canadian, 7, 9, 44, 47
Dollar, U. S.: convertibility into, 2; as intervention currency, 2; 1971 devaluation, 33; 1973 devaluation, 45-46, 109-10; whether it can float, 80
Dollar overhang, 38, 96, 100
Dollar standard: described, 2; Robbins views on, 24, 64; Haberler views on, 103-5; views summarized, 153
Double-digit inflation, 4

Elasticity of international demand and supply, 50-52, 60-61
Eurodollars, 12, 19, 41, 89-90
European Economic Community (EEC), 22, 84, 118, 124
European Monetary Agreement, 2
European monetary union, 20-22
European Payments Union (EPU), 2, 94-95
Exchange control, 132
Exchange rates: IMF rules, 2; fixed versus flexible, 4, 6, 65-66, 136, 157; Meade views on flexibility, 6; issues, 43-69; Clower views on flexibility, 65-66
Exporting inflation, 7, 9

Federal Reserve as lender of last resort, 90
Flexible exchange rates: Meade views on, 6; Robbins views on, 15-16, 20, 23, 157; Clower views on, 65-66; Cooper views on, 136. See also Floating exchange rates

161

SUBJECT INDEX

Floating exchange rates: and inflation, 9-10, 15; effects of, 20; case for temporary, 37; not wave of future, 58
Foreign aid versus foreign investment, 143-44
"Fork" proposal. See "Prong" proposal
General Agreement on Tariffs and Trade (GATT), 123, 125, 127
Germany, 7, 9, 30, 32, 33, 44, 49, 55, 56 150
Gold: Triffin views on, 3; conversion privilege ended, 7; role in reformed system, 38-39, 153-55; and numeraire, 109-10; two-tier system, 112-13, 114, 119; Cooper proposal, 115-16, 154
Gold standard: for central banks, 2; advocated by Rueff, 5; theory of, 17-19; and international adjustment, 92
Great Depression, 1, 43

Hague Conventions, 125

Import controls. See Import restrictions
Import restrictions: as alternative to devaluation, 51, 122, 127, 130, 131, 156
Import taxes. See Import restrictions
India, 136-37
Inflation: double-digit, 4; as global problem, 7; exporting of, 7, 9; and floating exchange rates, 9-10, 15; and devaluation, 44; in Canada, 47-48; national comparisons, 104-5
Inter-American Bank, 79
International adjustment. See Adjustment, international
International Development Association (IDA), 79
International Monetary Fund (IMF): intervention rules, 2; under Triffin Plan, 4-5; report on monetary reform, 12-13, 34, 72-73; future rules, 14, 22-23; as proposed keeper of ultimate means of settlement, 25; surveillance of temporary floating, 37; and Young proposal, 73-75; Articles of Agreement, 79, 115, 119; as proposed lender of last resort, 99; and Frank proposal, 100-1
International monetary reform. See Reform, international monetary
Intra-European arbitrage arrangement, 94

Japan, 7, 30, 33, 44, 55, 56, 104, 139

Keynes Clearing Union proposal, 2, 25
Korean War, 47

Laissez-faire in international arrangements, 15-16
Lender of last resort: and Federal Reserve System, 90; and IMF, 99

"Link" proposal, 9, 25-26, 40, 79-80, 100-1, 115-16, 154
Liquidity, international: feared shortage of, 4; not the problem, 5
Lira, 32

Malaysia, 80
Mexico, 80
Money illusion, 44, 48-50, 52-53, 68, 149
Multinational corporation, 41, 133

Netherlands, 55
Norway, 9
Numeraire, 90, 93, 107-9, 111-15, 152

Objective indicators, 35-37
Organization for Economic Cooperation and Development (OECD), 37
Overhang, dollar, 38, 96, 100

Phillips curve, 58
Pound. See Sterling
Price stability, 91
"Prong" proposal, 85, 86
Protectionism and devaluation, 128, 156
Purchasing-power guarantee for official dollar holdings, 105-7, 153, 155
Purchasing-power-parity theory, 148
Pyramid credit model, 81-84

Quantitative import restrictions, 132

Reconstitution of SDRs, 77, 78
Reform, international monetary: concern with since World War II, 1; postwar developments, 1-10; issues and choices, 11-27; official perspectives, 29-41; exchange-rate issues, 43-70; issues in design of, 71-119; trade issues, 121-32; problem of capital movements, 133-44; summary of conference dialogue, 145-57
Reserves, international monetary: explosion of, 6-7, 88; future form of, 24-26
Reserve unit proposal, 5, 6
Ricardian Law of Distribution of Precious Metals, 17

"Safeguard provisions" in U. S. trade legislation, 124-25
Sliding parity, 85
Smithsonian agreement, 14, 30, 31, 56, 59
Special drawing rights (SDRs): described, 6; not relevant to early 1970s, 8; proposed change in allocation, 9; convertibility of, 26; and dollar overhang, 38, 96-98; future of, 39-41; and Young proposal, 73-75; experience with, 76-78; possible reforms, 78-80; and issue of symmetry, 93; as possible intervention currency, 94; and EPU

SUBJECT INDEX 163

unit of account, 94; proposal to permit private holding, 95, 98; Douglass proposal, 96-98; Frank proposal, 100-1; and numeraire, 108-17; Cooper proposal, 115-16, 154; as substitute for gold, 140; as world money, 152-53
Sterling: 1972 speculation against, 32; 1967 devaluation, 45, 50-51, 149; 1949 devaluation, 47
Sweden, 9
Switzerland, 9, 32-33, 55
Symmetry as an issue, 35, 59-60, 64, 71, 93-94, 98

Trade issues in reform, 121-32
Triffin Plan, 4-5, 9

United Kingdom, 10, 14, 31, 149, 152
United States: and "deficits without tears," 5, 7; as exporter of inflation, 7, 9; and settlement of deficits, 38; and EEC, 84; need for payments surplus, 96; importance in global inflation, 104-5
U. S. balance of payments, 3-4, 7, 47, 56, 96-98
U. S. dollar. See Dollar, U. S.
U. S. Tariff Commission, 138

Variable levy of EEC, 124
Venezuela, 80

Working Party III of OECD, 37
World Bank, 25, 154
World War II, 1

Yen, 33, 56, 139, 140
Young proposal for international currency, 9, 73-75, 151-52